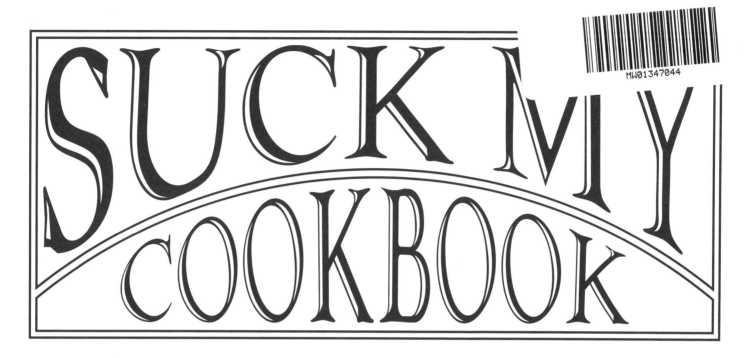

CLEAN RECIPES FOR DIRTY MINDS

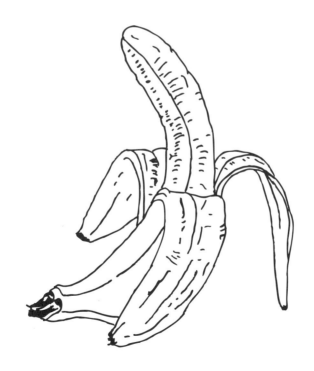

Suck My Press

Copyright© 2018 Seven Sisters, LLC

All Rights Reserved. No part of this publication may be reproduced, distributed, or transmitted in any form or by any means, including photocopying, recording, digital scanning, or other electronic or mechanical methods, without the prior written permission of the publisher, except in the case of brief quotations embodied in critical reviews and certain other noncommercial uses permitted by copyright law.

Published by Suck My Press, a division of Seven Sisters, LLC

For permission requests, write to the publisher, addressed, "Attention: Permissions Coordinator," at the address below:

Suck My Press
P.O. Box 3081
Alameda, CA 94501
www.suckmypress.com

ISBN: 978-0-9979437-0-2

Printed in Korea

Second Printing, 2018

Acknowledgements

We are fortunate to have quite an assortment of obscenely witty friends and family who encouraged us, brainstormed with us, and of course, suggested many toe-curling recipe ideas. Thank you so much to Lenny, Kirsten, Ken, Anne, Mark, CJ, Chris C., Dow, Alissa, Julie, Fred, Robin, Anna, Nicole, James, and Katie for helping us plan, cook, taste, film, strategize, publicize, and more. Most of all, thank you for sharing your dirty minds with us!

A special shout goes out to Kate for her lending her eagle-eyed proofreading prowess to the cause. You make us look good!

Finally, our undying gratitude goes to Big Daddy Bill, who appeared from Oz like a dream and generously shared his brilliant design skills with us. We were so lucky to have you!

TABLE OF

Appetizers

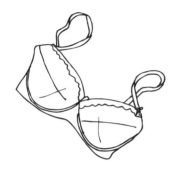

Savory Man Chowder 3

Why Don't You Fondue Me 5

Cockquitos & Guacahole 7

Hot & Creamy Cummus 11

Crudi-ta-tas 13

Pork Swords 15

Drinks

Pop My Cherry Punch 19

French Kiss Martini 21

Penis Coladas 23

Thai Me Up Mojito 25

Hot Buttered Rump 27

Money Shots 29

Dinner

Tagine de Vagine 33

Choke the Chicken Chili 35

Cuntry Pot Pie 38

Pull Out Pork Sandwich 41

Threeway Penne 43

Cunnilinguini 45

Jamaican Me Jerk Off Chicken 47

CONTENTS

Sides

Little Caesar Please Her 51

Num Num Titlets 53

Roasted Asparagus Shafts 55

Smell My Fingerling Potatoes 57

Sticky Nipple Rice 59

Dessert

Big Banana Flambé 63

Cream Your Pants Puffs 65

Pound the Pudding Pie 69

Cock Sucker Pucker Cake 71

Up the Butterscotch Brownies 73

Whip It Mousse 75

Breakfast

Sticky Buns 79

Morning Orgy Muffins 81

Manly Mancakes 83

Slammin' Ham 'n Eggs 85

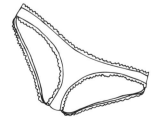

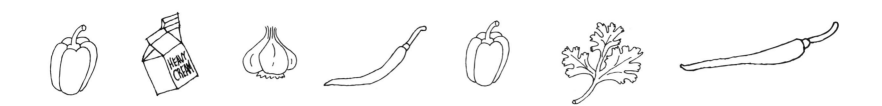

ARE YOU

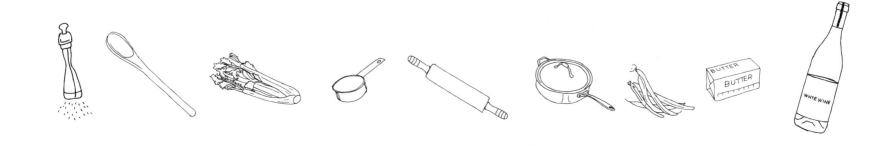

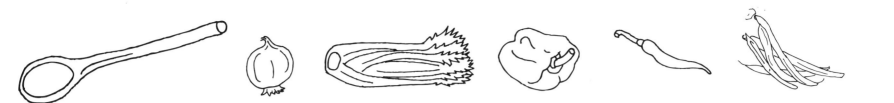

HUNGRY?

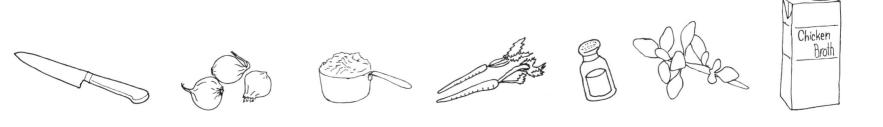

One of these is not like the others

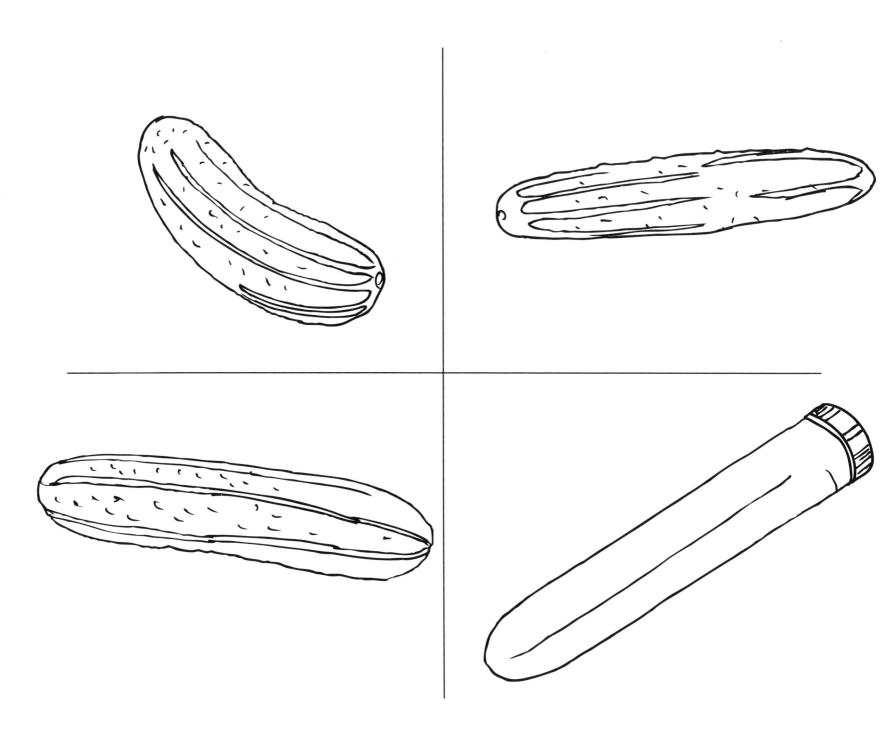

One of these is just not the same

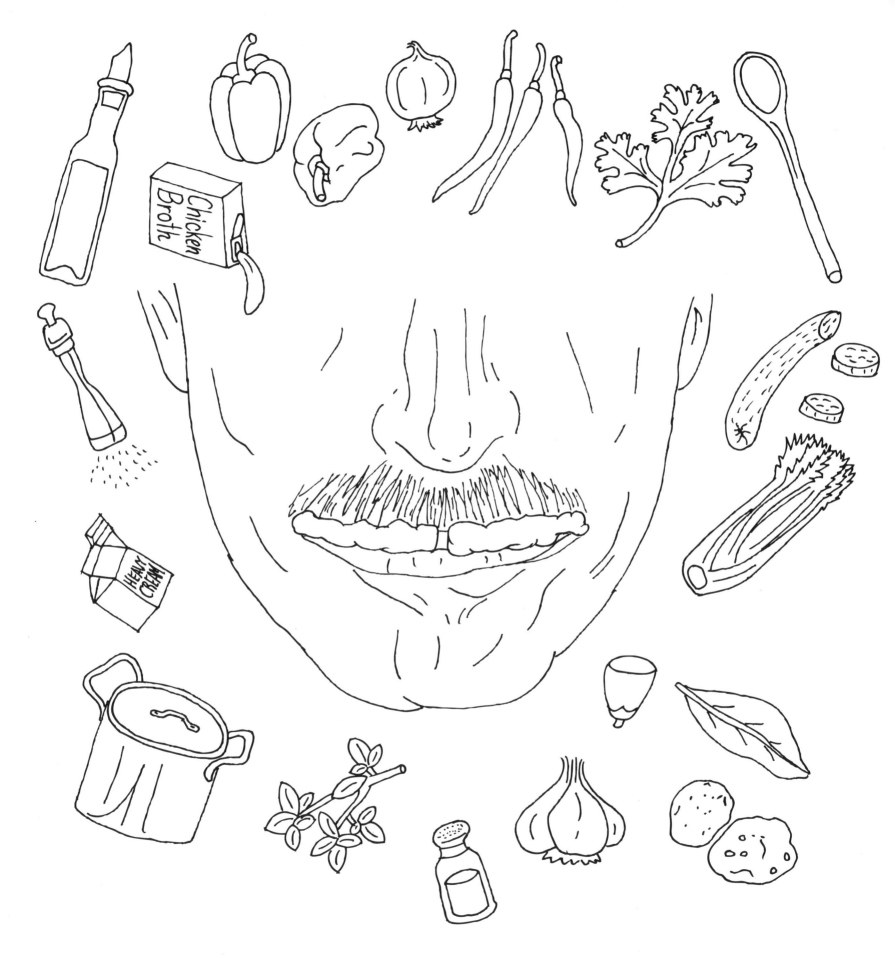

Savory Man Chowder

When the weather gets chilly and you long to swirl your breadstick in some silky warmth, whip up a pot of this hearty soup. All at once sweet, savory and just a bit salty, you'll enjoy swallowing load after hot load of this thick, creamy man chowder.

Ingredients

- 2 tablespoons olive oil
- 1 coarsely chopped medium onion
- 1 cup diced celery
- 1 chopped green bell pepper
- 1 chopped red bell pepper
- 2 cloves garlic, minced
- 1/2 teaspoon cayenne pepper
- 1 pound andouille sausage, diced
- 3 cups corn, fresh or frozen
- 2 bay leaves
- 2 teaspoons dried thyme
- 1 teaspoon paprika
- 6 cups low-sodium chicken broth
- 6 Yukon Gold potatoes, cut into 1/2-inch cubes
- 1 cup heavy cream
- salt and ground black pepper to taste
- 1/2 cup chopped cilantro

Directions

Heat olive oil in a large pot over medium-high heat. Cook onion, celery, and bell peppers, stirring frequently until softened, about 5 minutes.

Add garlic, diced andouille sausage, and cayenne pepper. Continue to cook and stir until the sausage is hot, 1 to 2 minutes more.

Add corn kernels, bay leaves, and thyme. Allow the mixture to simmer until the corn is warmed through, about 1 minute.

Add chicken broth and bring the mixture to a boil. Reduce heat and simmer, stirring occasionally, for about 30 minutes.

Stir in potatoes and heavy cream. Continue simmering, covered, about 20 minutes or until potatoes are tender. Remove bay leaves. Spoon out about 1 cup of the potatoes and broth into a blender and puree. Stir the puree back into the pot - this will make the man chowder nice and thick. Season with salt and pepper.

Dish into serving bowls and garnish with cilantro. For some lighthearted fun with your lover, take turns swishing your sausages to coat them in creamy man chowder, then lick it off. Delicious!

Why don't you fondue me?

A slow cooker will keep the heat going all night long, so get your long fork ready!

Optional accoutrements to this dish include a shag rug, a blazing fireplace, and a good compilation of 70's love songs... with bonus points for Barry White.

Ingredients

12 ounces each of Gruyère and extra-sharp cheddar cheese, grated
3 tablespoons flour
1 cup white wine, such as Chardonnay
¼ teaspoon ground nutmeg

Items for dipping, cut into bite-sized pieces: assorted breads, pretzels, sausage, raw or blanched vegetables such as bell pepper, cherry tomatoes, asparagus, broccoli, cauliflower, and zucchini.

Directions

Toss cheese with flour and place in slow cooker with wine and nutmeg.   (Please note: ingredients should fill the crock at least halfway; if not, increase recipe as needed. We are planning for an evening full of burning passion, not burning fondue.)

Cover and cook 45 minutes on the high setting until cheeses melt.

Stir, switch to low, and serve with the bread, vegetables, and other items.

Choose your morsel, then pierce it with your big fork and plunge into the hot, silky cheese. Be sure to lick every last drop of creamy goodness.
Pierce, plunge, eat, lick. Then do it again... pierce, plunge, eat, lick.
Give yourself over to the sweet rhythm... let it be your first, the last, your everything.

COCKQUITOS Y GUACAHOLE

Cockquito is the fake Spanish diminutive of the word cock, literally meaning little cock. These savory little stiffies will provide a tasty diversion when you can't get your hands (or mouth) on the real thing.

Ingredients

1 teaspoon vegetable oil
½ green bell pepper, chopped
½ onion, finely diced
2-ounce can roasted and peeled green chiles, finely diced
¼ teaspoon dried cilantro
2 cloves minced garlic
1 pound skinless, boneless chicken breast, cut into 1-inch pieces
1 batch homemade taco seasoning
    (1 tablespoon chili powder, ¼ teaspoon onion powder, ¼ teaspoon garlic powder, ¼ teaspoon crushed red pepper, ½ teaspoon dried oregano, ½ teaspoon paprika, 1 ¼ teaspoon ground cumin, 1 teaspoon sea salt, 1 teaspoon ground black pepper)
¾ cup water
12-14 corn tortillas
½ cup shredded Cheddar cheese
1 cup salsa
24 toothpicks
2 cups vegetable oil for frying

Directions

Heat 1 teaspoon vegetable oil in a skillet over medium heat. Stir in the onion, garlic, chiles, and bell pepper and cook until they have softened, about 5 minutes.

Increase heat to medium-high and stir in the chicken breast. Stirring frequently, cook about 10 minutes or until the chicken breast is no longer pink in the center.

Shred the chicken using two forks, then stir in the spices and water. Simmer until the liquid has evaporated, stirring occasionally, about 10 minutes. Sprinkle in the cheddar cheese, then remove from heat, and set aside.

Warm the tortillas for a few seconds in the microwave to soften. Lightly brush each corn tortilla with a layer of salsa. Spread about 2 tablespoons of the chicken mixture in a line along the bottom edge of the tortilla. Tightly roll the tortilla into a cylinder, and secure the ends with one or two toothpicks. Repeat with remaining tortillas.

Heat 2 cups vegetable oil in a large skillet to 375º F (190º C).

Fry the cockquitos in the preheated oil, no more than 4 at a time, until golden and crisp, about 4 minutes. Drain them and discard toothpicks. Pair finished cockquitos with your favorite guacahole. We like the sweet and savory recipe that follows.

SWEET AND SAVORY GUACAHOLE

And while you can always top them with a quick squirt of sour cream, cockquitos are even more fun when plunged deep into a creamy guacahole. If you like, you can begin with your fingers - dip one or two into the guac's silky depths, creating a slick channel. Withdraw your fingers, lick them clean, grab your cockquito and dive in!

Ingredients

4 ripe avocados, peeled and pitted
1 large mango, peeled, pitted, and chopped
1 small red onion, minced
4 limes, juiced (separated)
2 serrano chile peppers (or to taste)
sea salt to taste
¼ cup chopped fresh cilantro

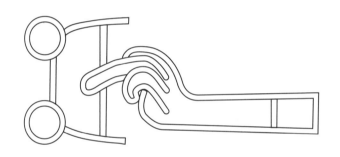

Directions

Combine the onion and the juice of 2 limes and allow them to mingle for at least an hour. Strain the onions and set aside. (The juice will take the bite out of the raw onions. Of course, if biting is your thing, simply skip this step.)

Grind the chile peppers, the juice of the other 2 limes, and salt together in a food processor until no large chunks of pepper remain. Add 1 avocado and process until creamy and smooth; repeat with remaining avocados. Transfer the mixture to a serving bowl. Fold the onion, cilantro, and mango into the avocado mixture. Serve at room temperature - a cold dip might wilt your hot cockquito!

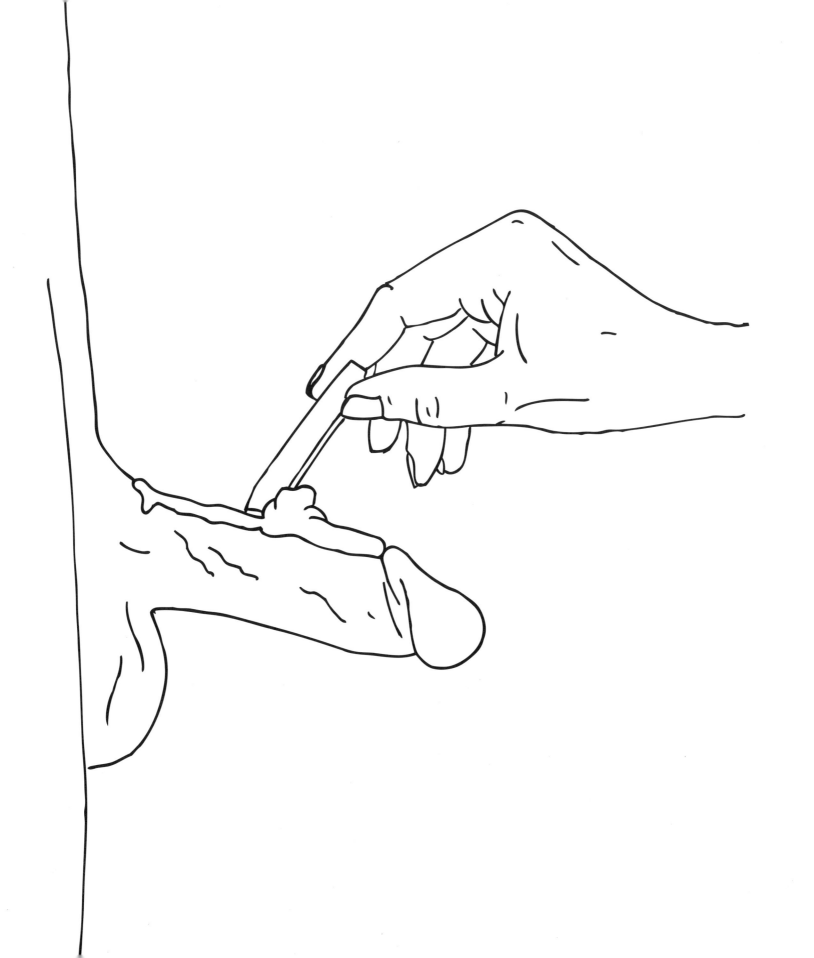

Hot and Creamy Cummus

Dip your carrot stick into this slick, luscious cummus
and prepare to lick it all off - or invite someone else to!
Greek yogurt gives it a smooth, velvety texture, cayenne pepper
brings the heat, and the lime juice will pucker your puss.
And the best part? This cummus is nice and light, so you can sink
your stick all night long - no need to rest between dips.

Ingredients

¾ cup fat-free plain Greek yogurt
1 15-ounce can chick peas
2 cloves garlic
2 tablespoons lime juice
1 tablespon sesame oil
1 teaspoon ground cumin
1 pinch cayenne pepper
1 tablespoon extra, extra virgin olive oil
1 pinch paprika

Directions

Drain and rinse chick peas, then drop in blender. Add all other ingredients, puree until smooth and creamy, and start dipping!

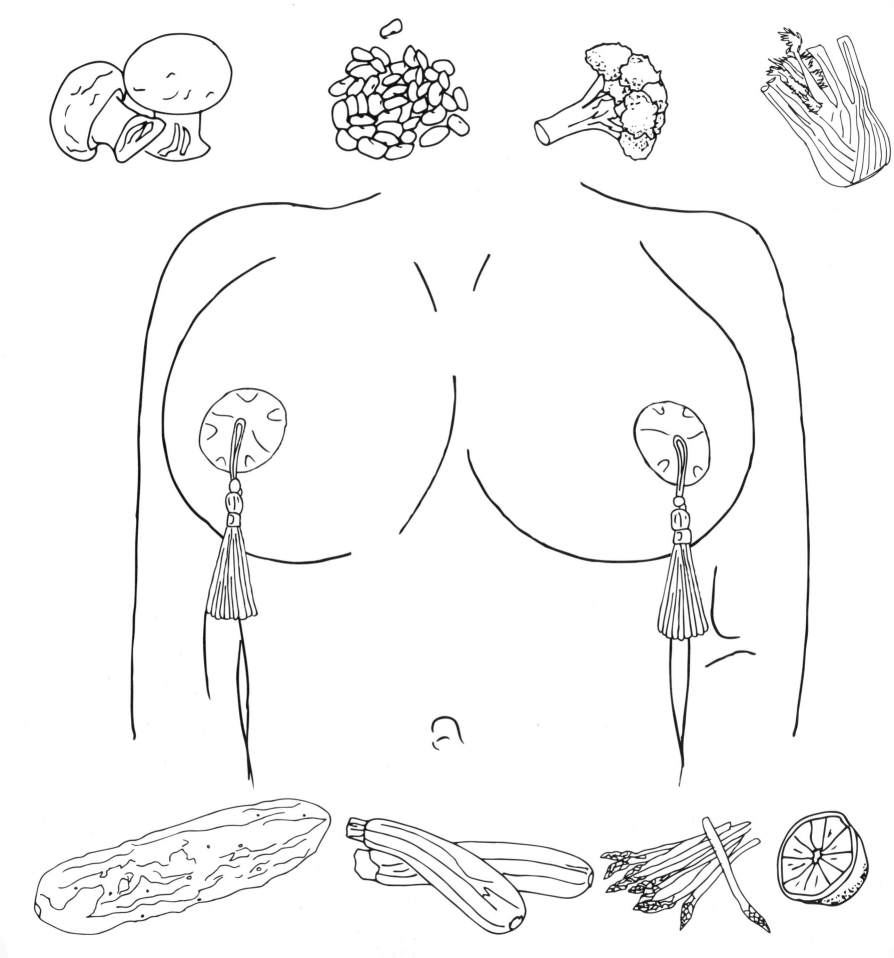

Crudi-ta-tas

Dip it raw! Sculpted white bean dip forms the centerpiece of this dish: a set of scrumptious, round ta-tas. Titty-titty yum YUM!

Large or small, soft or firm, crudi-ta-tas can vary quite a bit, and we urge you to play with your options. Will you surround your white bean ta-tas with cherry tomatoes that explode in the mouth? Petite but pleasingly firm cornichons? Tender, round, slightly salty baby potatoes that simply beg to be licked? Don't limit yourself, and your crudi-ta-tas will be the talk of the party!

Ingredients

Vegetables sliced for finger-dipping. Suggestions include cucumbers, carrots, celery, cherry tomatoes, bell peppers, broccoli, mushrooms, olives, boiled baby potatoes, zucchini, fennel, and asparagus (see "A Note About Asparagus" on page 55).

3 15-ounce cans cannellini beans, rinsed and drained
Note: if your tastes run to ta-tas of color, substitute your choice of black beans, rose beans, or yellow chick peas.
3 cloves crushed garlic, or to taste
⅓ cup olive oil
2 lemons, juiced
1 teaspoon kosher salt
1½ teaspoon white pepper (or to taste)

Directions

Prepare the dip. In a food processor or blender, combine the beans, garlic, olive oil, lemon juice, salt and pepper. Process until smooth. Add more salt and pepper as desired.

To assemble, place two small dishes in the center of a serving platter and overfill the dishes with dip to form soft, round mounds. (Don't worry if one is slightly larger than the other - it's perfectly natural, and it won't stop anyone from enjoying them.) Once you have sculpted the ta-tas into the size and shape that pleases you, add the finishing touch - one plump olive in the center of each.
Finally, surround those mounds with vegetables and let the dipping begin!

Pork Swords
Crispy Prosciutto-Wrapped Asparagus Shafts

Challenge your lover to a duel before dinner, and make pork swords your weapon of choice! Select your asparagus shafts carefully for ideal girth and firmness, about ¾- to 1-inch thick, to ensure nice, stiff swords. Avoid pencil-thin shafts as well as old, tough shafts that have lost their flexibility. Wrap each snugly in a sheath of tender prosciutto and broil to salty, porky, crispy perfection. One or two shafts won't be enough to satisfy, so make it an orgy!

Ingredients

1 tablespoon olive oil   16 spears fresh asparagus, trimmed*   16 slices prosciutto

Directions

Preheat the oven to 450º F (230º C). Line a baking sheet with aluminum foil, and coat with olive oil.

Starting at the base, wrap one slice of prosciutto around and around each asparagus shaft, spiraling all the way up to the tip. Repeat with the remaining spears, leaving space between each on the baking sheet. Avoid crossing swords - if they touch at this stage, you could end up with disappointingly soft, flaccid shafts.

Bake for 5 minutes in the preheated oven. Remove, shimmy the pan back and forth to let the shafts roll about, then return to the oven for another 5 minutes. Remove when the asparagus is tender and the prosciutto is crisp, and serve while hot.

*See "A Note About Asparagus" on page 55

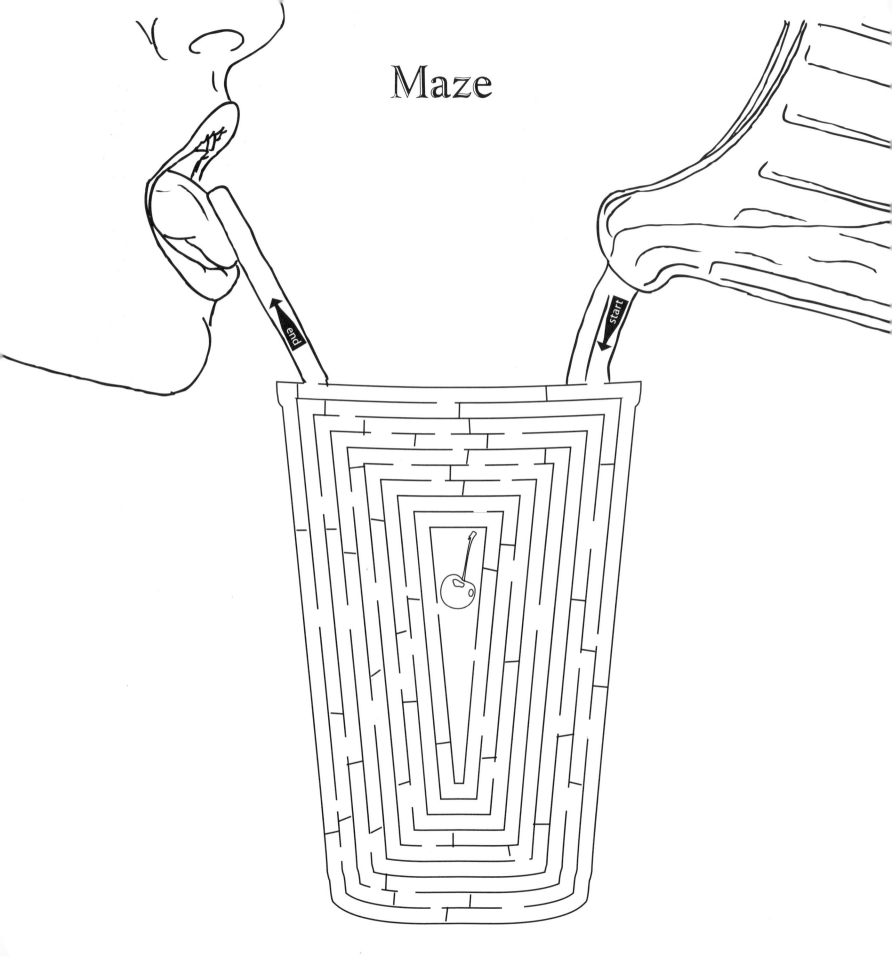

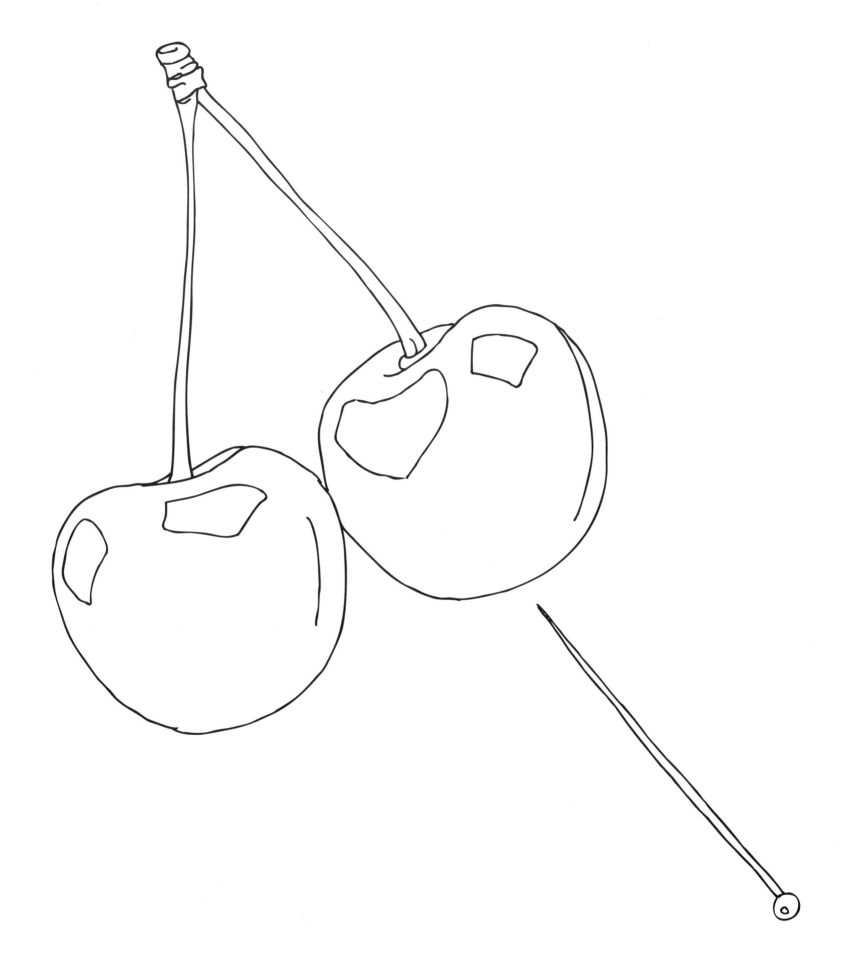

My Cherry Punch

THE KEY TO THIS RECIPE IS SELECTING CHERRIES THAT ARE RIPE AND READY TO BE POPPED. LOOK FOR A FULL BODY AND A DEEP ROSY FLUSH.

INGREDIENTS

- ½ pound fresh sweet cherries
- 6 tablespoons agave, separated
- Triple sec to cover cherries (Cointreau works well)
- 6 ounces bourbon
- 4 cups soda water

DIRECTIONS

Wet the cherries and remove stems. Pour 2 inches triple sec in a clean glass jar and add 2 tablespoons of agave. Put the fruit in the jar to marinate, and add more triple sec if needed to fully cover the cherries. You want them really wet and dripping.

Cover and marinate for 3-7 anticipation-filled days. Finally, once they are thoroughly soused, you are ready to pop these cherries! Remove them from the triple sec, set the liquid aside and place the cherries, one at a time, in a mortar and pestle.

Every cherry is unique, and you can explore different ways to pop each one. You can simply pound until it bursts open. You can slowly roll the pestle against the cherry, gently coaxing it until it offers up that pit. Or simply use your fingers to delve in. Once you have popped all those wet cherries and discarded the pits, it's time to mix up the punch, one sweet cup at a time.

Add 1½ ounces bourbon, 1 cup soda water, 1 teaspoon agave and ¼ of the cherry-infused triple sec to an ice-filled cocktail shaker and shake. Pour punch into a glass over ice, topping it with ¼ of the cherries. For even more cherry-popping fun, use a drink sword to prick each fruit.

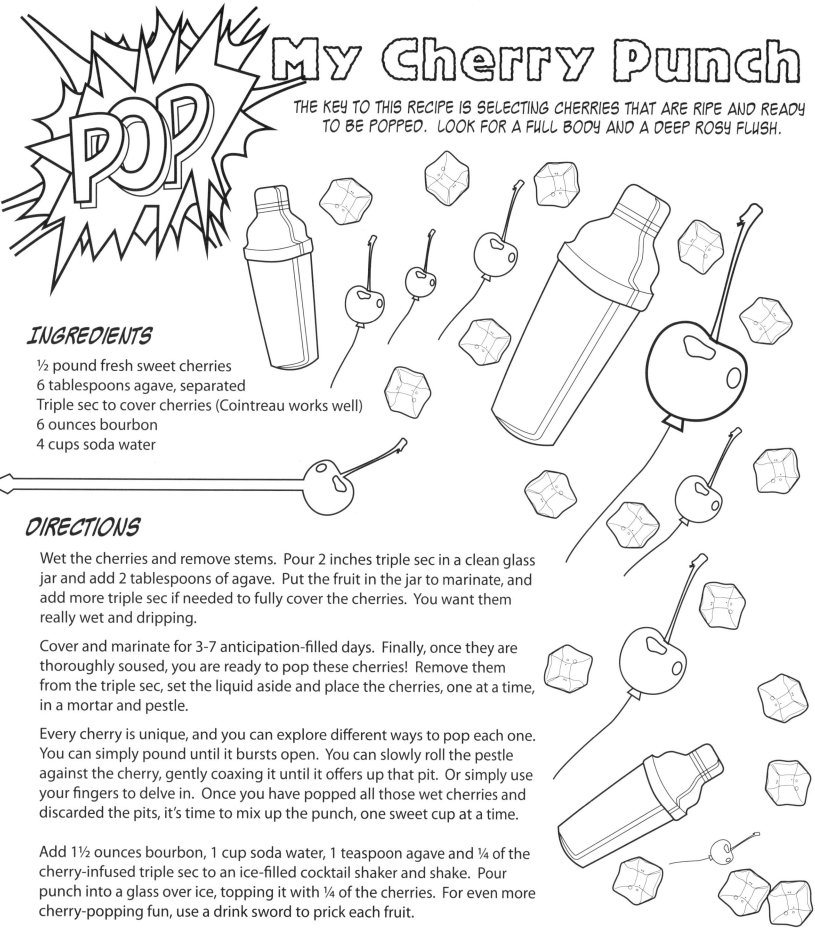

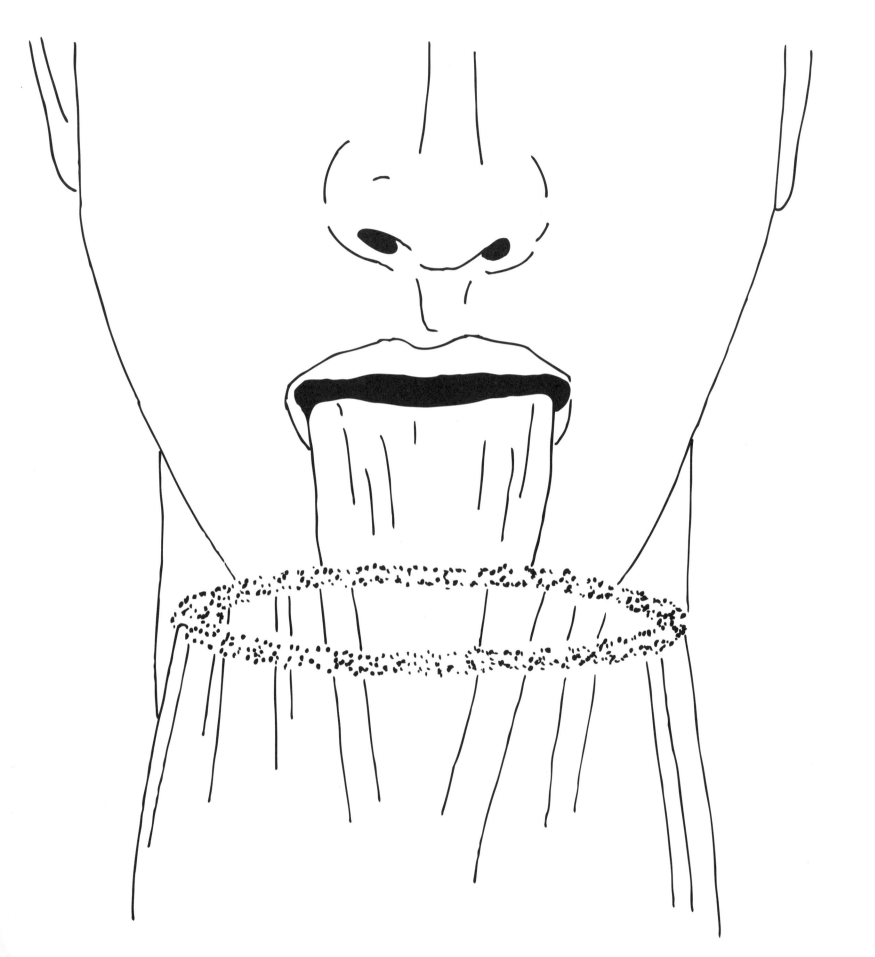

Sweet Rim French Kiss Martini

Ingredients

2 ounces vodka (we prefer Tito's)
1 ½ ounce chambord
1 ½ ounce pineapple juice
1 slice lemon or pineapple
Rimming sugar (or regular sugar in a pinch)

Directions

In a cocktail shaker or tumbler,
mix drink ingredients and shake with ice.

To sugar the rim:

1. Pour sugar onto a plate. Make sure the sugar forms a ring that is bigger than the glass.

2. Twirl the fruit slice around and around the mouth of the glass, moistening the rim. Rub with care, and don't rush. Taking your time and fully priming the rim makes the drink much more satisfying for both the giver and the receiver.

3. Turn the glass upside down, press firmly into the sugar, and pull straight up. Nothing fancy here - rolling and twisting will make an uneven rim.

4. Now that your rim is ready and waiting, pour the mixed drink in and sip away. Have fun playing around the rim - you can swirl, lick, flick, poke and probe it with your tongue, and even use your teeth to very, very delicately scrape some of that sweet rim sugar straight into your mouth. Just let your impulses flow, and relish how exhilarating rimming can be.

Penis Coladas

Rumor has it that pineapple makes cum taste sweet.
IS IT TRUE?
Suck down a few of our special Penis Coladas and find out!

Chubby Penis Colada

The coconut cream makes this tropical concoction extra thick and velvety. On those days when you are feeling decadent and just need a bit... more, the Chubby Penis Colada will fill you up like nothing else.

Ingredients
2½ ounces golden rum
3 ounces pineapple juice (unsweetened)
1 ounce coconut cream
5-6 ice cubes

Directions
Blend ingredients on high, adding ice cubes one at a time.
Garnish with a cherry or pineapple slice.

Skinny Penis Colada

Yes, girth is important, but this recipe proves that a skinny penis can also tickle the right spots. The magic is all in what you do with what you've got, so for best results use fresh pineapple and take the time to blend. If it must be a quickie, however, you can substitute pineapple juice and serve it on the rocks.

Ingredients
½ cup pineapple (preferably fresh)
½ cup crushed ice
3 ounces coconut rum

Directions
Blend ingredients on high until smooth.

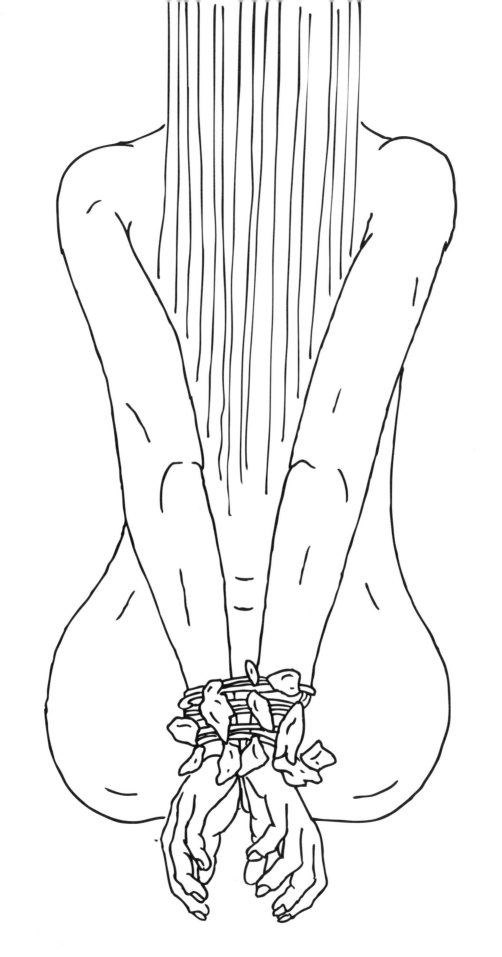

Thai Me Up

Coconut-Ginger Mojito

฿3,000

Exotic, sweet and spicy, this little number will transform any bedroom into Bangkok.

Ingredients
2 ounces ginger-infused coconut rum
1 cup soda water
4-5 fresh mint leaves
Agave for added sweetness if desired

Directions
Muddle or tear the mint leaves and scatter them in a cocktail glass with ice. Pour the coconut-ginger rum over the leaves, then add the soda water for a bubbly climax. Stir, serve, and sip your way to your own happy ending!

To make the ginger-infused coconut rum:
Slice 1/4 cup of fresh ginger and slip it into one 750ml bottle of coconut rum (we like Parrot Bay). Let sit for at least 24 hours before using. Whatever coconut-ginger rum you don't use on the spot can be kept in your liquor cabinet for future use.

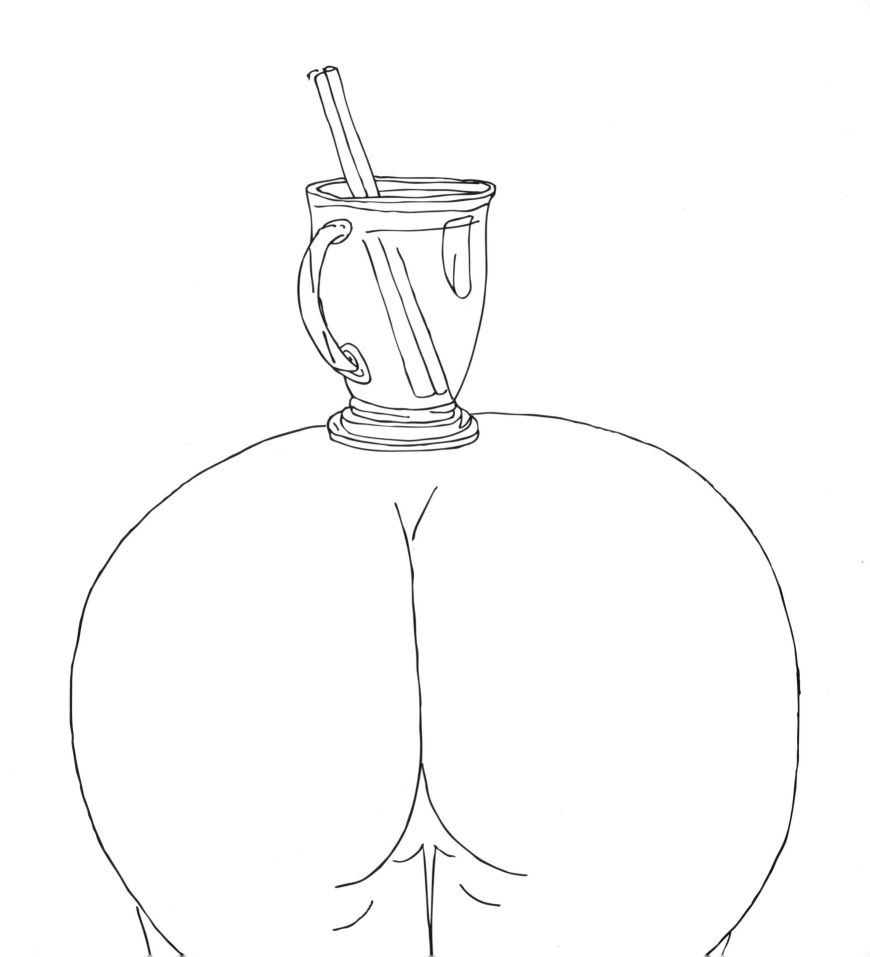

Hot Buttered Rump

Keep this luxurious lubricant warm in your slow cooker and you'll keep them coming back for more... and more... and more!

Ingredients

2 cups dark brown sugar, firmly packed
½ cup unsalted butter
1 teaspoon salt
½ teaspoon ground nutmeg
1 pinch ground allspice
⅛ teaspoon ground cloves
3 cinnamon sticks
1 vanilla bean
8 cups hot water
2 cups light rum
Whipped cream
Ground cinnamon

Directions

Mix all ingredients except rum in slow cooker and set on warm for 5 hours.
Stir in rum just before serving.
Top each Rump with a squirt of whipped cream and a sprinkling of cinnamon.
Bottoms up!

THE BLOW JOB

Sources disagree on the origins for the name of this shot. Some say it comes from the tradition of drinking them hands-free, lifting the glass with a steady jaw and plenty of suction from the lips.

Others say that it's due to the way the whipped cream flecks around the sides of the mouth as the drinker sucks down every sticky drop of the luscious liquid.

And some say it's because serving a Blow Job increases your odds of getting one.

Bottom line: you can't go wrong!

Ingredients

½ ounce Irish creme liqueur
½ ounce coffee liqueur
½ ounce amaretto
Top with an enticing mound of whipped cream

Directions

Pour the ingredients one at a time, directly into the shot glass, in the listed order - and invite your guest to open wide.

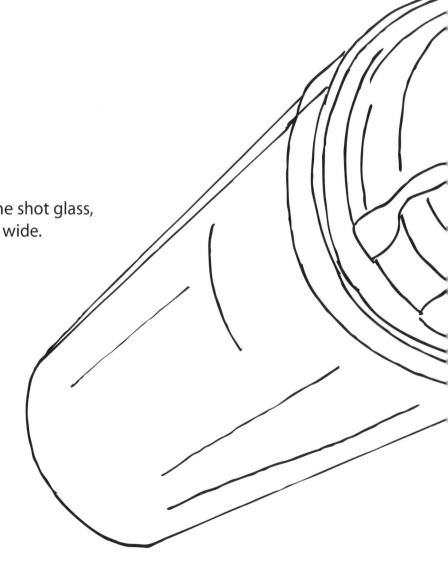

THE WET PUSSY

This delicately flushed pink shot gets ready fast and goes down easy.

Just add 5 drops of strawberry cream/tequila liqueur (such as Tequila Rose) to 1½ ounce butterscotch Schnapps and soak it up!

SHOTS

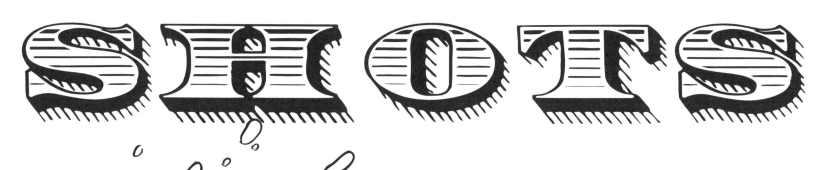

SWEET COOTER SHOOTERS

So sweet and sticky, only a sugarholic aphrodesiate could swallow them. So order one for your bosom buddy and if they drink it, enjoy the honey pot you just found!

Ingredients

¾ ounce ginger-infused coconut rum
(see page 25 for instructions on infusing your rum)
¾ ounce chocolate liqueur (we like Godiva)

Directions

Combine the rum and the chocolate liqueur and enjoy!

THE JIZZER

This 3-ounce shot is meant to overflow the shot glass so you can watch your favorite cum guzzler lick it off the sides - or shoot the overflow straight from the cocktail shaker into your partner's open, waiting mouth.

Ingredients

1 ounce vodka
2 ounces white chocolate liqueur

Directions

Shake over ice and serve dripping wet.

In the mood for some rimming?
Double the recipe, serve as a martini, and be sure to rim the glass with white chocolate shavings to keep those tongues wagging. (Learn all about rimming on page 21.)

Find the Differences

Can you spot all 15 differences?

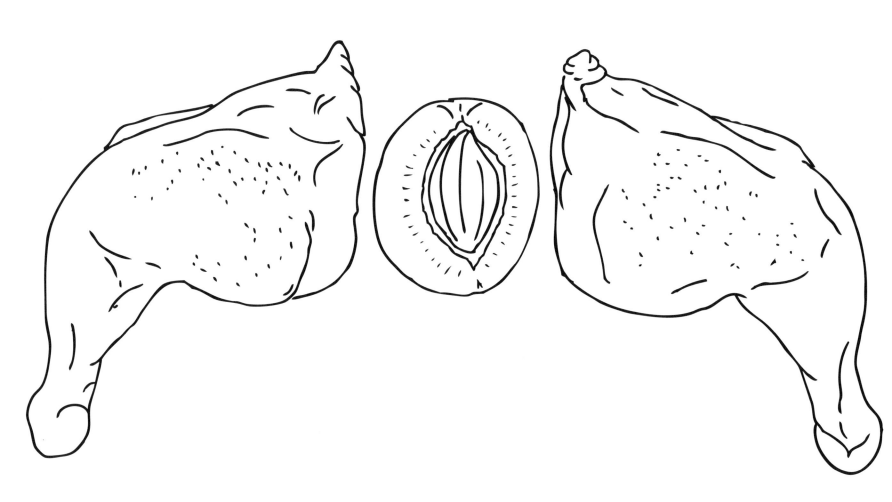

Tagine de Vagine

With so much sweet and spicy goodness, you'll want to bury your tongue deep in this dish. Lap up the honey sauce drizzling down a tender thigh... make gentle, swirling circles at the center of a plump, juicy apricot... and flick sharply against the smooth nub of a skinless almond.

But please... once you've started, you'd better not stop until this Vagine is finished!

Ingredients

- 6 pounds chicken thighs
- 1 large yellow onion
- 2/3 cup butter
- 1/2 teaspoon turmeric
- salt to taste
- 1 teaspoon black pepper
- 2 cinnamon sticks
- 1 pound dried apricots
- 3 tablespoons honey
- 2 teaspoons ground cinnamon
- 1/2 cup peeled almonds
- 1 tablespoon sesame seeds
- 1 tablespoon vegetable oil (to sauté the almonds)

Directions

In a large pot, melt the butter and sauté the onions until soft and glistening.

Add the chicken, salt, pepper, turmeric and cinnamon sticks. Add enough water to cover the chicken, about two cups. Bring to a boil, reduce the heat, and simmer until the chicken is done, adding more water if necessary. Remove the chicken pieces and set aside.

Add the apricots to the sauce and simmer for about fifteen minutes, then add the ground cinnamon and honey. Stir and simmer until the sauce thickens. Add more honey to achieve the thick, sticky consistency desired - or if you simply like your Vagine extra sweet.

When the sauce is almost there, quickly sauté the almonds in oil. Remove the nuts, then drain most of the oil and use the same pan to quickly toast the sesame seeds. Place the chicken back in the sauce to reheat.

Arrange thighs on a platter and drizzle the hot, sticky sauce all over them. Top with the almonds and the sesame seeds. Serve with couscous.

Peeling your almonds

The puckered, wrinkly skin of an almond against our tongues can be delightful, but sometimes we prefer them naked, smooth and silky. To peel your almonds, simply submerge them in boiling water for exactly one minute, run them under cool water and voila! The skin has softened, and you can gently - so, so gently - rub the nub between your fingers to loosen the skin and reveal the sleek, naked almond beneath. Don't lose control, though. Rub too hard, and you may find that you have shot your almond all the way across the room.

Choke the Chicken Chili

Consider this dish a reliable stand-by... perfect for those times when you feel the hunger and just need some quick and easy (yet still smoking-hot) satisfaction. For the most intense payoff, be sure to start with spice and get the chicken really hot before you pull it.

Ingredients

- 2 tablespoons olive oil
- 1 red bell pepper, diced
- 1 small onion, chopped
- 1 teaspoon chipotle chili powder
- 1 teaspoon ancho chili powder
- 2 teaspoons cumin
- 2 teaspoons ground sea salt
- 2 cloves garlic, minced
- 1 tablespoon dried oregano
- 1 can black beans, rinsed and drained
- 1 can white beans, rinsed and drained
- 1 can pink beans, rinsed and drained
- 1 28 ounce can diced tomatoes
- (Choose low-sodium beans and tomatoes when possible)
- 2 pounds chicken breast
- Salt & pepper to taste

Directions

In a heavy-bottomed pot or slow cooker, warm the olive oil over medium heat, then sauté the onion and bell pepper until slightly softened and golden, about 4 minutes. Some call this sweating the vegetables, but the real heat comes when you add the chipotle, ancho, and cumin powders next, stirring them gently until fragrant - about 1 minute.

Add the salt, oregano and garlic and cook about 1 minute, taking care not to burn the garlic. Add the diced tomatoes with their juice. Then add the rinsed and drained beans and stir, gently at first and then a bit more vigorously as things begin to come together. Nestle the chicken breasts into the mixture and bring to a boil, then cover and simmer for 1.5-2 hours in a pot, or 3-4 hours on high in a slow cooker.

When the breasts are white and pull apart easily, it's time to choke the chicken! Use a slotted spoon to transfer the chicken to a plate, then pull it apart with a fork or your fingers, bit by bit, until it completely comes undone.

Return the shredded chicken to the pot, and, if needed, simmer uncovered to reduce the liquid. Salt and pepper to taste and serve over rice or quinoa.

If you freeze the leftovers in individual servings, you'll have quickie lunch or dinner fulfillment at your fingertips for whenever you need some solo satisfaction.

CUNTRY POT PIE

Few things are more red-blooded American than that icon of farmhouse kitchens, the rich and creamy, wholesome and hearty chicken pot pie. So wiggle into those Daisy Dukes and push your tits up to the sky with a snugly-knotted tight plaid shirt... because tonight, you're the farmer's daughter - and you're serving it up cuntry-style!

Pie Crust

Ingredients

1¼ cup flour
¼ teaspoon salt
10 tablespoons unsalted, very cold butter, cut into small pieces (about ¼ inch)
2-4 tablespoons ice water

Directions

Pulse flour and salt in a food processor to blend. Sprinkle the bits of butter evenly over the dry mix and pulse until it forms little balls (or, if you're lucky, big balls). Wet them with 1 tablespoon of the ice water and pulse. Repeat 1 tablespoon at a time, but no more than 4 total until the dough is just moist enough to stick together, but not wet or sloppy. (The creamy filling will come later.)

Empty dough onto a lightly-floured surface and quickly shape into a ball, then flatten the ball into a disk. Cover it tightly with plastic wrap and refrigerate for at least 2 hours. Roll it out on a lightly floured surface into your desired shape for baking.

Chicken Filling

Ingredients

5 tablespoons unsalted butter
1 small onion, diced
2 large carrots, diced
1 large celery stalk, diced
½ cup flour
3½ cups low-sodium chicken stock
¼ cup white wine
¼ cup half & half
½ cup fresh green beans, chopped
¾ cup corn kernels, fresh or thawed
1 teaspoon ground sage
1 teaspoon ground thyme
salt and pepper to taste
3 cups cooked chicken, diced or shredded

Directions

Melt butter over medium heat. Sauté onions, carrots and celery 7-8 minutes, until very light gold. Add wine and cook until liquid is reduced by half. Stir in flour until evenly distributed and cook for 1-2 minutes. Slowly whisk in chicken stock until sauce is smooth. Add half & half, bring to a boil, then reduce heat and simmer for 6-8 minutes to thicken sauce. Stir in green beans, corn, and chicken. Salt and pepper to taste and remove from heat.

Preparation

If you have a mix of pussy lovers and cockophiles on your guest list, you can delight them all by making individual pies tailored to their preference.

Preheat oven to 425° F (220° C).

Roll your pie crust out to ⅛ inch thick on a lightly floured surface. Keep the dough cool and avoid overworking. If it warms up, it will start to stick to the rolling pin.

Place a ramekin on the crust and cut a circle that leaves ½ inch extra around the dish. Use this method to make 4 mini pie crusts. Save the remaining dough for decoration.

Spoon the pie filling into 4 10-oz buttered ramekins or oven-safe dishes. Make sure the filling does not come all the way to top of the outer lip of the dish or you will get soggy crusts.

Cover each ramekin with a round top. Pinch the excess overflow around the edges to form a traditional outer pie crust.

Top each crust with a cock, a steamy slit, or one of each.

To make pussy pie, ventilate the crust with a steamy slit. Cut a medium slit in the center of the pie, then fold the crust along one side of the slit to form a left labia. Shape a thin piece of extra pie crust into a right labia and place along the other side of the opening. Pinch the right and left lips together at the top and bottom of the opening to ensure you get the appropriate shape. For added realism, shape additional pieces of crust to form a clit, and an outer left and outer right labia. Lightly pinch pieces together at the seams where they adhere. No additional steam vents are needed for these pies.

To make a crusty cock, start by creating the penis head and shaft out of dough. Cut two fat ovals to make the balls, then attach the balls to the bottom of the shaft. Place the cock on the center of your pie and poke 4 small slits around the outside. Finally, cut the main steam-releasing slit in the center of the cock head.

Once you have topped your pies, glaze them with egg wash to get a shiny, golden look when baked. Beat an egg with 1 teaspoon of milk and brush lightly over crusts. Pay special attention to your decorations and apply a bit of extra wash to key spots for an extra-glistening look.

Bake

Place a sheet of aluminum foil on the center rack of the oven and preheat to 375° F (190° C).

Set pies on top of the foil in the oven to catch the juicy drippings that may burst forth when things get hot. Bake 20-30 minutes until golden brown, then rest for 5 minutes on a cooling rack. Your pies are now ready to be ravished!

Rocky Mountain High:

In states where it is legal to do so, you can literally put the pot in Pot Pies and intoxicate your guests!

Simply follow the traditional pie crust recipe above, replacing the regular butter with cannabis-infused butter (commonly reefer-ed to as cannabutter, weed butter, or pot butter). Be sure to have extra munchies at hand!

Pull Out Pork Sandwich

You know that you can have lots of naughty fun by pulling out and showering liquid pearls all over your partner's _____ (insert favorite body part here).

But let's be honest - when you HAVE to pull out, it can be a drag. Let this sweet, salty, hot and juicy sandwich bring you back to the edge of bliss… because you can pack this bun with as much pork as you like, and you're allowed to revel in it all the way to the end.

Ingredients

- 4 pounds cubed pork shoulder with visible fat trimmed off
- 1 tablespoon ground thyme
- 1 tablespoon ground sage
- 1 teaspoon salt
- 1 medium onion, chopped
- 4 cloves garlic, minced
- 1 bottle hard apple cider
- 1 pink lady apple, peeled and sliced
- 1 granny smith apple, peeled and sliced
- Pepper to taste
- Cranberry goat cheese (or dried cranberries and plain goat cheese)
- Arugula
- Kaiser rolls

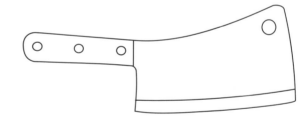

Directions

Coat pork in herb mix and put in slow cooker. Add onion, garlic and cider. Cook on low for 8+ hours. Add the sliced apples for the final hour of cooking. If you don't have a slow cooker, you can use a Dutch oven; cook for 2-3 hours at 325º F (165º C). Shred pork with two forks.

To make the sandwich

Cut rolls in half and spread generously with cranberry goat cheese. Pile it high with juicy pork and apples, and top with a handful of arugula. Dig in - and don't stop until you're done!

Penne Three Way

You'll never forget your first penne-tration! Fresh hot pasta, tender young peppers and a big juicy sausage dripping in sauce make this dish a steamy three-way for your mouth!

Ingredients

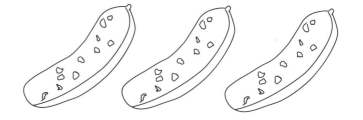

1 pound penne pasta
1 pound Italian sausage, cut into 1-inch pieces
½ teaspoon crushed red pepper flakes
2 teaspoons Italian seasoning
   *you can use pre-made or make a batch yourself by combining 1 teaspoon each dried basil, oregano, rosemary, marjoram, cilantro, thyme, savory and red pepper flakes and blending in a food processor.
3 cloves garlic, chopped
1 small onion, chopped
1 green pepper, cut into strips
1 red or yellow pepper, cut into strips
½ cup red wine (merlot or pinot noir)
6 ounces tomato paste
8 ounces tomato sauce
15 ounces crushed tomatoes
1 teaspoon sugar
½ teaspoon salt
¼ cup Parmesan cheese
½ cup fresh basil, chopped
salt and pepper to taste

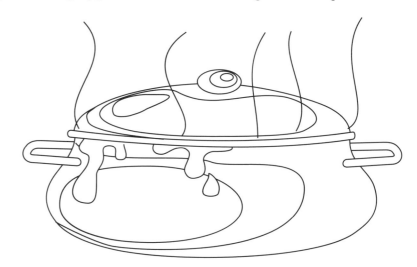

Directions

Boil pasta until al dente in a pot of heavily salted water. Cook sausage in a large skillet over medium-high heat 15-18 minutes or until lightly browned and no longer pink.

Add red pepper flakes, Italian seasoning, garlic, onion, and peppers; sauté for 5 minutes or until onions and peppers have softened.

Add wine, tomato paste, tomato sauce, crushed tomatoes, sugar and salt. Cover and simmer for 10 minutes.

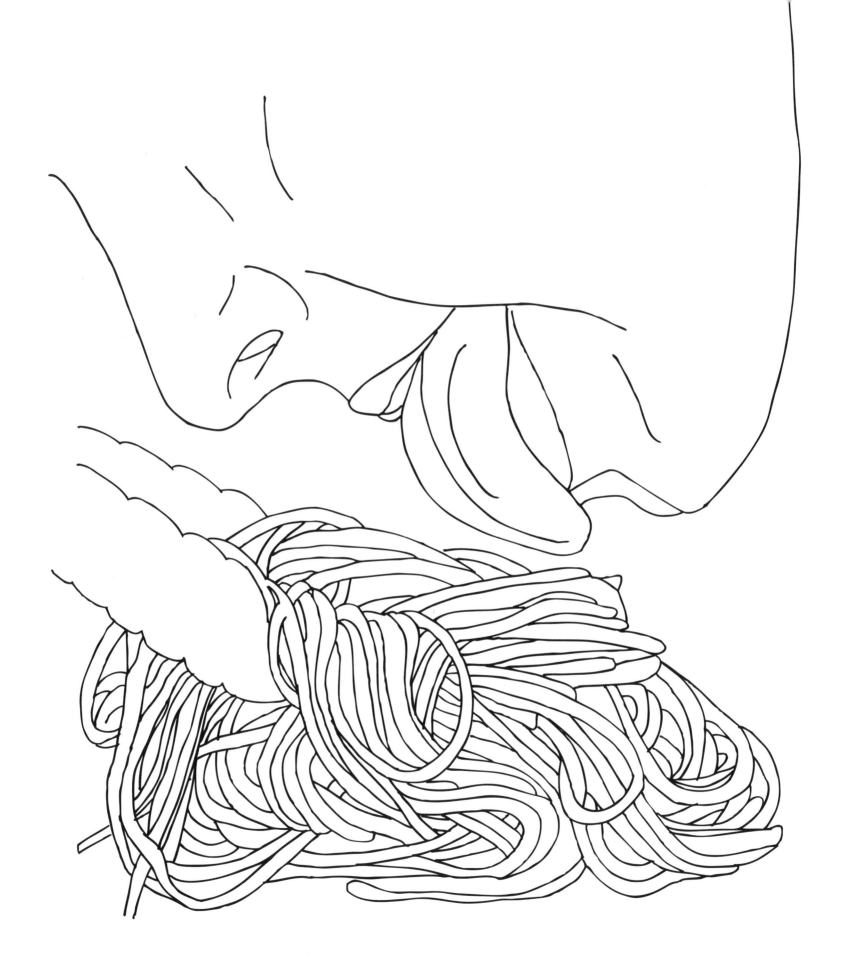

Cunnilinguini

Wet and dripping, you'll find this hot mound of pasta is an irresistible enticement for the tongue. You'll want to lick and nibble these tender folds over and over again, as each stroke electrifies your senses and curls your toes. So dive right in and lap up every last delectable drop!

This recipe is open to improvisation... a swirl (of lemon juice) here, a pinch (of red pepper flakes) there… whatever tickles your fancy - and that of your dining companion, of course. Try swapping thyme or basil for the parsley, or just add them on top. And if you have a penchant for red over white, add your favorite tomatoes - fresh, saucy or crushed.

Ingredients

1 16-ounce package linguini
2 8-ounce cans minced clams with juice, or 2½ cups fresh clams, mussels or shrimp
¼ cup olive oil OR 3 tablespoons butter, or combination
2-3 cloves garlic, minced
¼ cup fresh parsely, finely chopped
¼ cup dry white wine
½ teaspoon salt
¼ cup Parmesan cheese

Directions

Bring a large pot of heavily salted water to a rolling boil, then add linguini and boil until al dente. We're going for a soft yet firm sensation for the tongue, so don't overcook! Drain pasta and set aside.

In a large skillet, sauté the garlic in the olive oil. Stir continuously while adding the clam liquid, parsley, white wine, and salt. Continue to cook for 10 minutes or until sauce thickens to desired consistency, then stir in clams until heated through. (If using fresh clams, add them to the pan, then cover and cook until the shells open. Dispose of any that don't open!)

Toss cooked and drained linguini with the clam sauce and Parmesan, and serve hot!

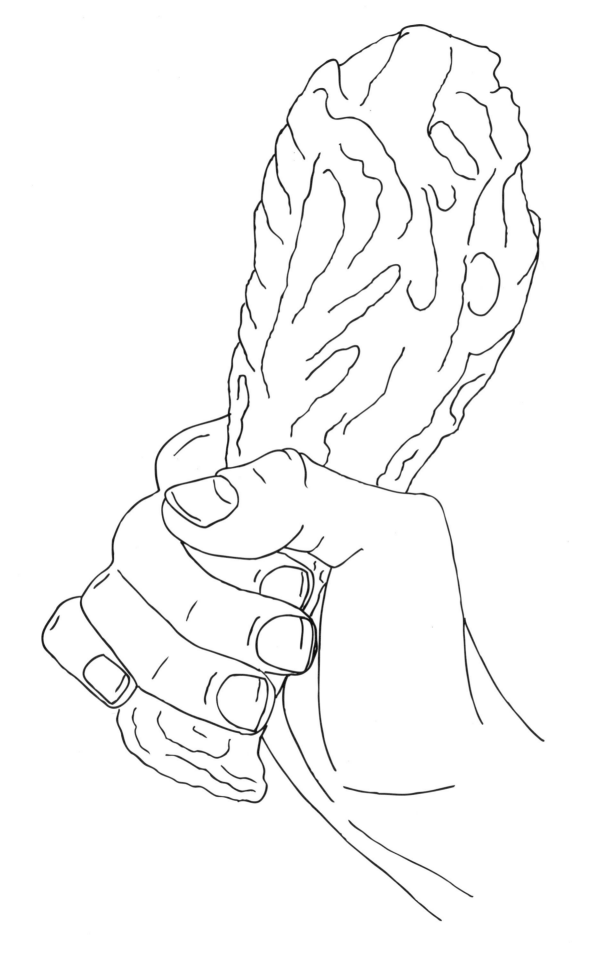

Jamaican Me Jerk Off Chicken

We like a quick and easy jerk, so this recipe departs a bit from tradition. Using boneless chicken breasts and store-bought seasoning mix make it so simple that you can cook jerk with one hand... while jerking whatever you like with the other.

Ingredients

Jerk seasoning, enough to coat chicken
¼ cup lime juice
1 pound boneless chicken breasts
1 fresh pineapple cut into spears
2 green or red peppers, cut into strips

Directions

Rub the breasts with jerk seasoning. Place them in the lime juice (putting chicken, seasoning and juice all in a gallon-size plastic bag works well) and allow to marinate in the fridge for a minimum of 4-6 hours. When they are good and soused, toss the breasts on the grill along with the pineapple and peppers.

Grill chicken 5-6 minutes per side, then remove it to a serving platter or plate and top with the grilled pineapple and peppers.

See "A Note About Asparagus" on page 55 and fork an extra pineapple spear if you suffer from an asparagusic funk to your spunk!

Word Search

```
X D C K S N U B Y K C I T S C B X L Y S
R F H G U A C A H O L E R T A E O Z W C
E M O R N I N G O R G Y M U F F I N S J
S E K A C N A M S C Y V X X O G E F N U
C R E A M Y O U R P A N T S P U F F S R
V S T I C K Y N I P P L E R I C E O K Z
I T H A I M E U P Q N M K Z A Q W K O T
F R E N C H K I S S M A R T I N I R O M
C O C K Q U I T O S G K L S V B L E B M
X Y H S D R O W S K R O P B S L J J K A
E N I G A V E D E N I G A T T U D E O N
W X C C U M M U S T O H S Y E N O M O C
X O K T P O P M Y C H E R R Y P U N C H
E M E B M A L F A N A N A B G I B A Y O
Q D N U M N U M T I T L E T S B W C M W
S I C R U D I T A T A S P H M E Y I K D
A W H I P I T M O U S S E N B R T A C E
I N I U G N I L I N N U C N U A Q M U R
M S L X A J F P E N I S C O L A D A S D
M E I P T O P Y R T N U C Y B J T J L P
```

BIG BANANA FLAMBÉ
CHOKE THE CHICKEN CHILI
COCKQUITOS
CREAM YOUR PANTS PUFFS
CRUDITATAS

CUMMUS
CUNNILINGUINI
CUNTRY POT PIE
FRENCH KISS MARTINI
GUACAHOLE

JAMAICAN ME JERK OFF
MANCAKES
MAN CHOWDER
MONEY SHOTS
MORNING ORGY MUFFINS

NUMNUM TITLETS
PENIS COLADAS
POP MY CHERRY PUNCH
PORK SWORDS
STICKY BUNS

STICKY NIPPLE RICE
SUCK MY COOKBOOK
TAGINE DE VAGINE
THAI ME UP
WHIP IT MOUSSE

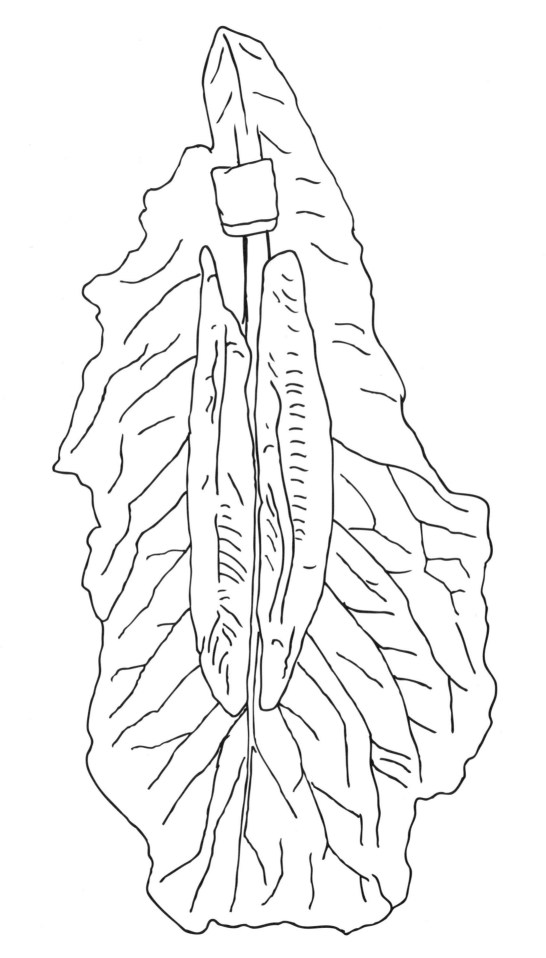

Little Caeser Please-Her

Each of these mini Caesar salads double as faux pussies, so snatch the opportunity to hone your oral expertise. Eat it up and down, nibble from one end to the other, or simply lap up the slick dressing and suck down the anchovy. Any extra croutons can be used for extended laser-focused clit-flicking workouts. Your lady friends will be well pleased, indeed!

Salad

Ingredients

1 head Romaine lettuce
1 jar or tin of oil-packed anchovies
Croutons and dressing

Separate the individual Romaine leaves, wash thoroughly and pat dry. Lay them out on a platter and place one anchovy lengthwise on each, labia-style. Drizzle the dressing and get them dripping wet. Finally, position a crouton clit on one end of the anchovy.

Now you have a platter full of faux pussy, all lubed up and ready to be munched!

Croutons

Ingredients

3 thick slices French bread, cut into ¼ inch cubes
2 tablespoons butter
1 clove garlic, minced
salt and pepper to taste

Preheat oven to 375º F (190º C). Melt butter in a small saucepan over medium heat, then add the garlic and stir for about 2 minutes.

Arrange French bread cubes in a single layer in a baking pan, and pour butter mixture over the bread cubes. Season with salt and black pepper, and toss to coat.

Bake 5-10 minutes or until lightly browned on the outside, and crisp in the middle.

Dressing

Ingredients

2 tablespoons lemon juice
1 tablespoon Dijon mustard
1½ teaspoon Worcestershire sauce
1 teaspoon kosher salt
1 clove minced garlic
fresh ground black pepper to taste
⅓ cup olive oil

Place all ingredients except olive oil in a bowl and whisk together. Slowly drizzle in olive oil while whisking lemon mixture with the opposite hand until emulsified.

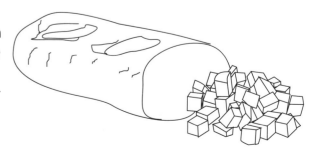

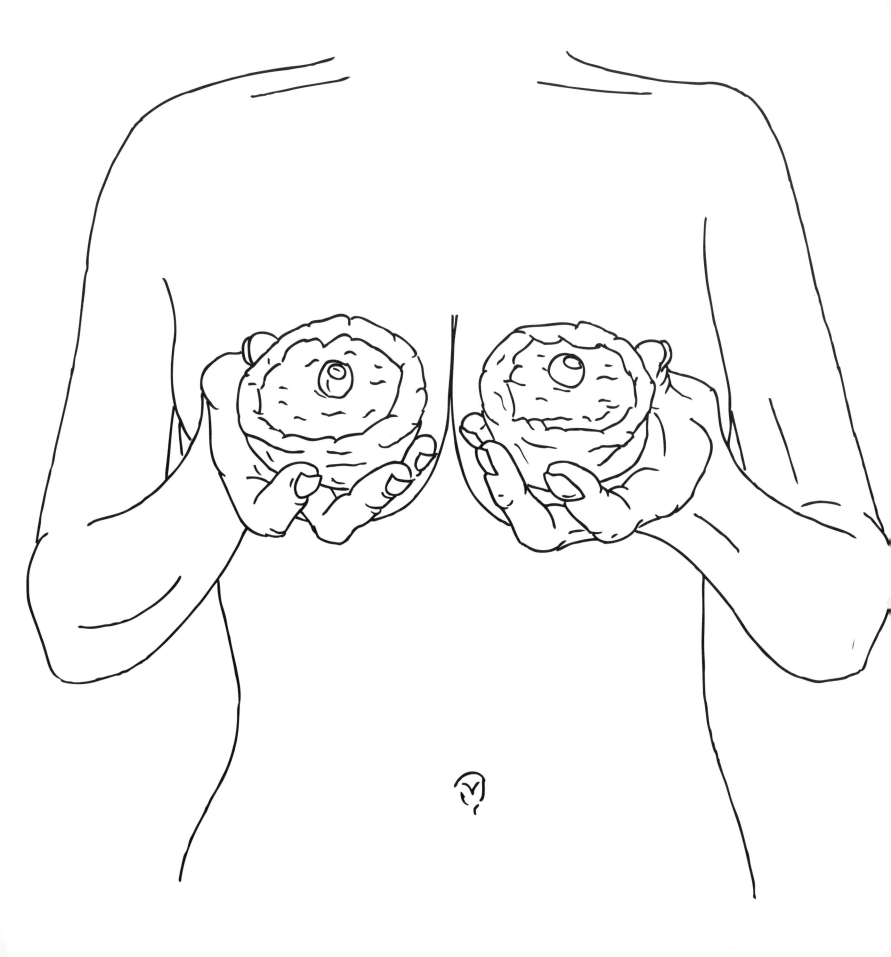

Num Num Titlets

Puffy, petite, and downright adorable, these savory little pastries make the perfect mouthful!

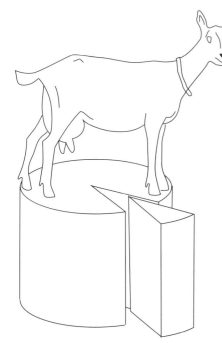

Ingredients

1 package (14 ounces) frozen puff pastry sheets
2 tablespoons olive oil
1 tablespoon lemon juice
1 tablespoon fresh basil, chopped
¼ teaspoon salt
½ teaspoon black ground pepper
1 egg, lightly beaten
1 cup walnuts, chopped
11 ounces goat cheese
9 pitted black olives, cut in half the short way

Directions

Heat oven to 375º F (190º C) and remove pastry from freezer. While it thaws, combine the olive oil, lemon juice, basil, salt and pepper in a bowl and whisk until emulsified.

Unwrap the puff pastry and cut out 9 rounds from each sheet, using a biscuit cutter. (If you don't have one, press the top of a drinking glass into the dough and cut around it with a sharp knife.) If enough dough remains, roll it out and make 1 or 2 more rounds.

Now use a slightly smaller cutter or a knife to make a light dent in each round, creating a rim. Use a fork to make a few pricks in the center of each pastry; this will prevent the center from rising, while letting the outer rim puff up. Place them on a baking sheet and brush the egg on each pastry, around the edges only.

Evenly distribute the chopped walnuts in the center of each round, and then drizzle about ½ teaspoon of the basil mixture over them. Add a dollop of goat cheese on top - enough to spread evenly within each cup to and fully cover the nuts and basil; this will result in smooth, irresistible titlets.

Finally, top each with ½ of a black olive to simulate the nipple - and stimulate your tongue!

Cook for 18 - 20 minutes, until the cheese is melty and the pastry is puffed and golden brown. Cool slightly, then serve in pairs.

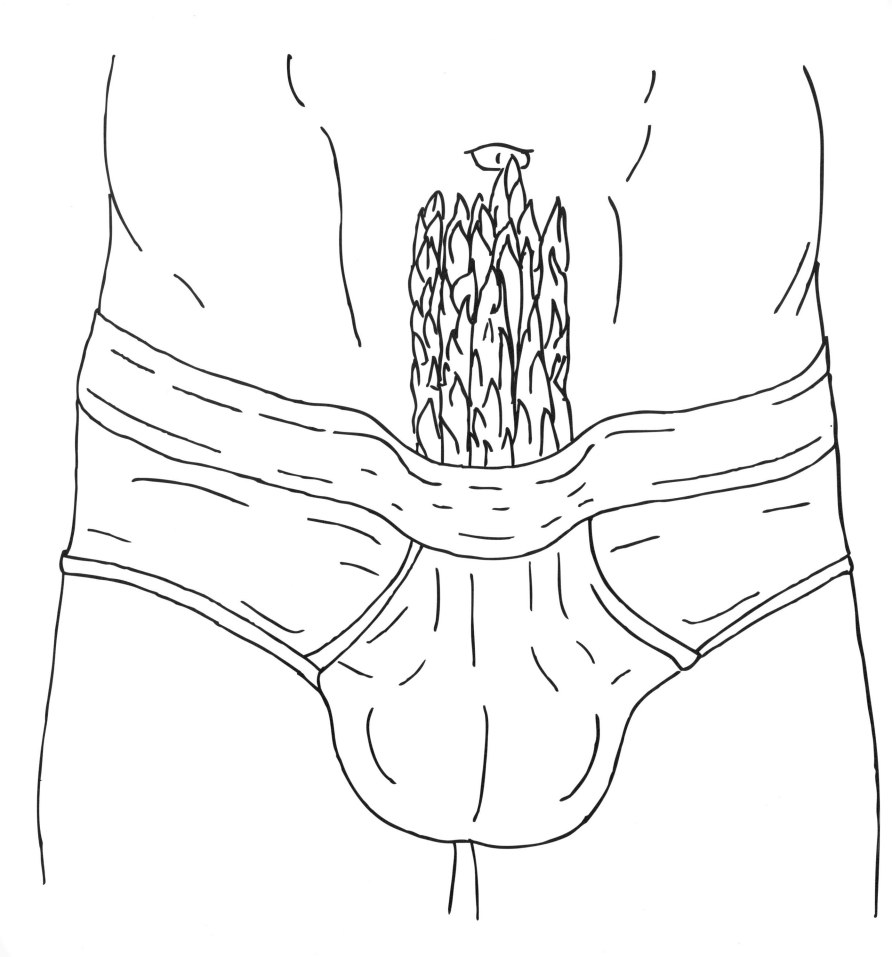

ROASTED Asparagus Shafts

When selecting your asparagus, always choose fresh and keep in mind that the thicker the shaft, the longer you can cook it without going soft.

Ingredients

2 pounds
fresh asparagus shafts

Olive oil

2 small red onions,
thinly sliced

2 teaspoons
chopped tarragon

Salt

Pepper

Directions

Preheat oven to 425° F (218° C).

Hold each shaft under running water and gently rub.
Stroke slowly and firmly from the base all the way to the tip.

Cut off the tough ends and lightly pat dry.
Most people love a nice, long shaft, but if you feel it will be too much of a stretch, simply cut each down to a manageable size.

Toss shafts with olive oil, tarragon, sliced red onions, salt and fresh ground pepper. Arrange in a single layer in a roasting pan.

Roast for 10 minutes.
Pay close attention for the subtle signs that indicate the shafts are ready.
When they are close... so close... the color will flush and deepen.
You may see small drops of condensation, especially at the tips.
This will be your cue that they are ready to come... out of the oven.

Finish with a squeeze (not too hard!) of fresh lemon over the shafts before serving.

A Note about Asparagus

Some male readers are gun-shy about serving asparagus when they know they'll be dishing out horizontal refreshments later on. They worry the famous pee-stank phenomenon caused by asparagusic acid might befoul their man-blast and spoil their date's appetite.

Have no fear! Our team of sexperts combined scientific research with plenty of tongue-on taste testing. While we confirmed asparagus can make for some pungent rod-rum, we also came upon a solution. Eating fresh pineapple takes the funk right out of your spunk. So serve up some Penis Coladas or grilled pineapple spears along with Roasted Asparagus Shafts and relax, knowing you'll enjoy oral delights at the table AND in the bedroom.

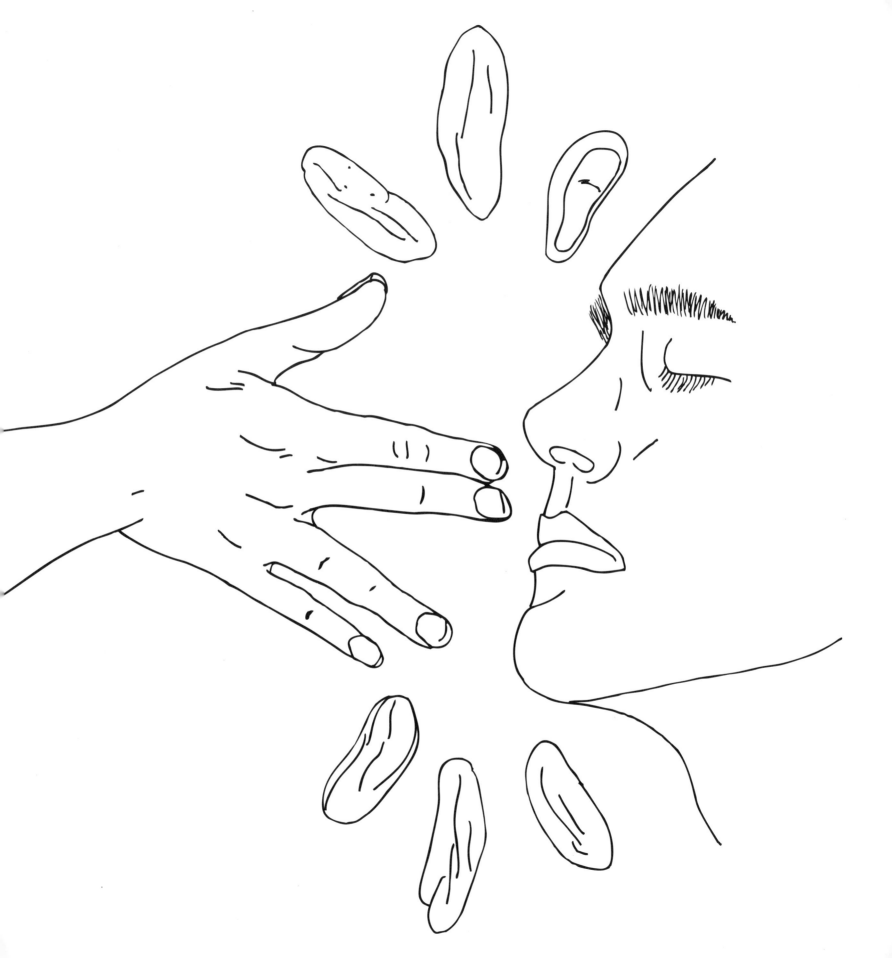

Smell My Fingerling Potatoes

Smell them, lick them, bite them, suck them!
There's no end of possibilities with these fingerlings –
there are so many different things you can do with them.

Here's one idea we like, but you can experiment and try any fresh herbs you have handy.
Just sniff first, and if it makes your mouth water, then give it a go!

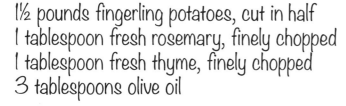

Ingredients

1½ pounds fingerling potatoes, cut in half
1 tablespoon fresh rosemary, finely chopped
1 tablespoon fresh thyme, finely chopped
3 tablespoons olive oil

1 teaspoon coarse sea salt
¼ cup Parmesan cheese, grated (optional)
2 cloves minced garlic
Pepper to taste

Directions

Preheat oven to 425° F (220° C).
Combine olive oil, garlic, rosemary and thyme and stir. Drizzle mixture over the potatoes, stirring to evenly coat them.

Place potatoes on a parchment-lined baking sheet and cook for 15 minutes. Remove from oven, salt and pepper to taste, and flip the potatoes. Bake for another 10 minutes.

Remove again, sprinkle with grated Parmesan cheese if desired, then place back in oven for 5 more minutes until it melts. If you like them crispy, place them under the broiler on high for 3-4 minutes, keeping a close eye on them so they don't burn.

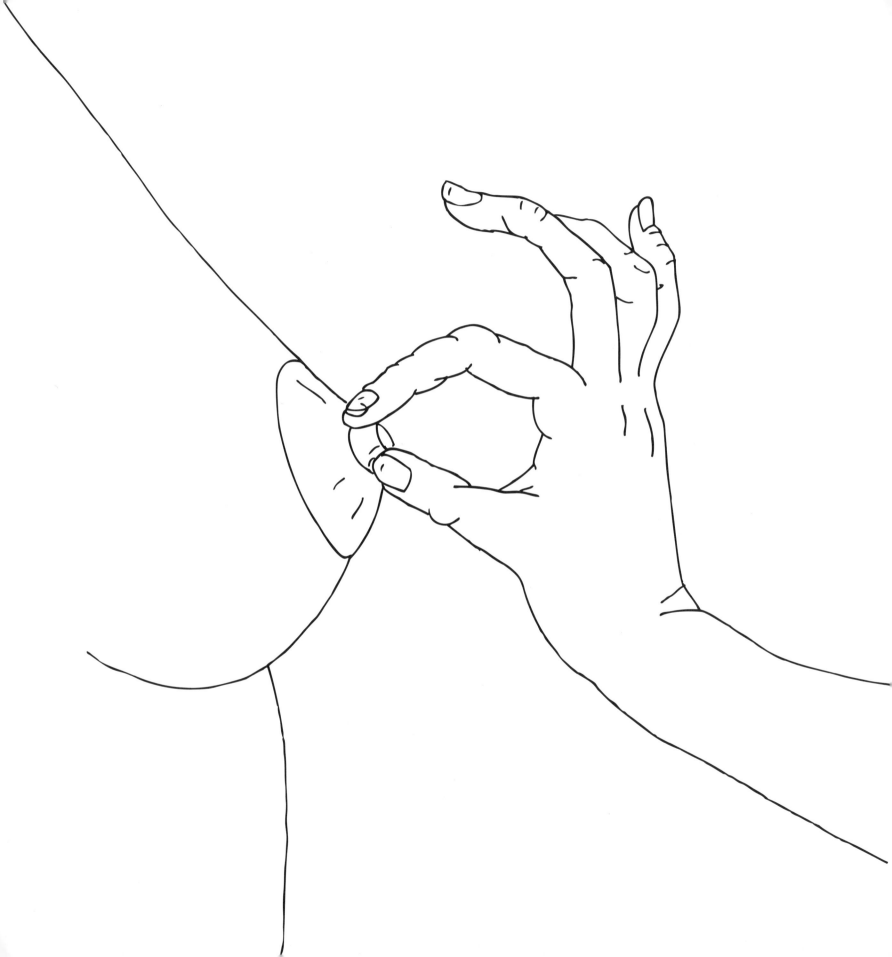

Sticky Nipple Rice

you'll just want to put it in your mouth!

ingredients
1 can coconut milk
(light or regular, depending on how heavy you like 'em)
1¼ cup water
1 teaspoon sugar
1 pinch salt
1½ cup uncooked jasmine rice
¼ cup shredded coconut (optional)
Mango chutney
Black sesame seeds

directions

Combine coconut milk, water, sugar and salt in a small pot, stirring until sugar dissolves. Add the rice and bring to a boil, then cover and reduce heat. Simmer 18-20 minutes - do not lift the lid lid or stir while rice is cooking. Add the shredded coconut at the end and mix it in as you fluff the rice with a fork.

To serve, mold the rice into your favorite shape of titty. Based on your personal preferences, use 1-2 teaspoons of mango chutney to form the areola on each and place the appropriate pinch of black sesame seeds in the center to shape the nipple.

Connect the Dots

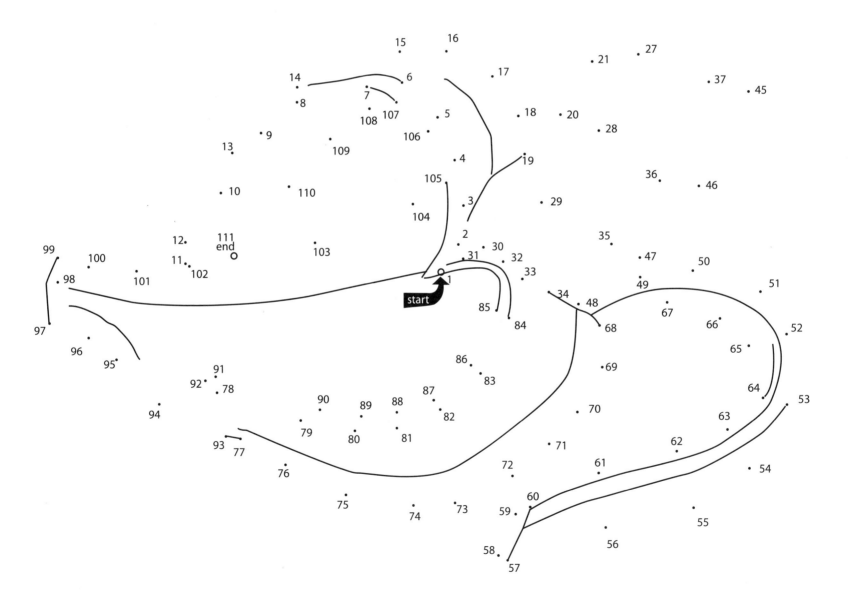

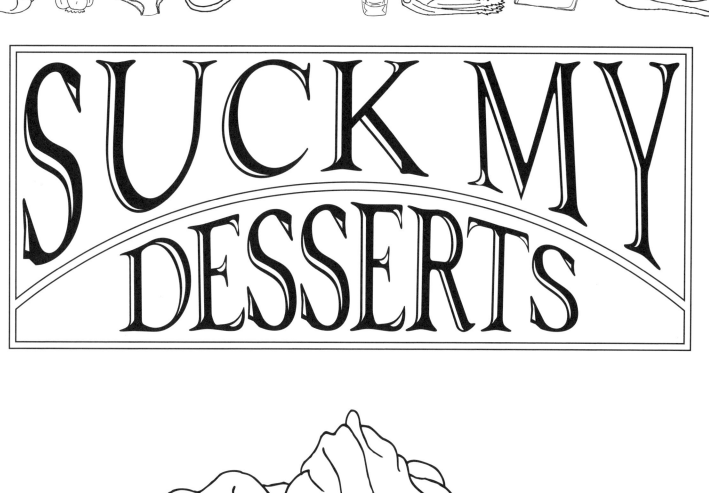
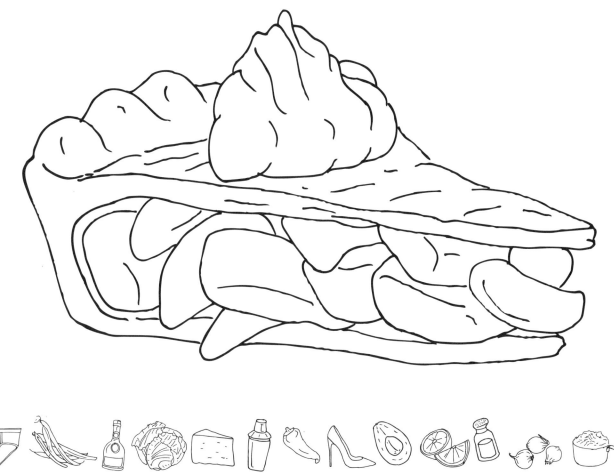

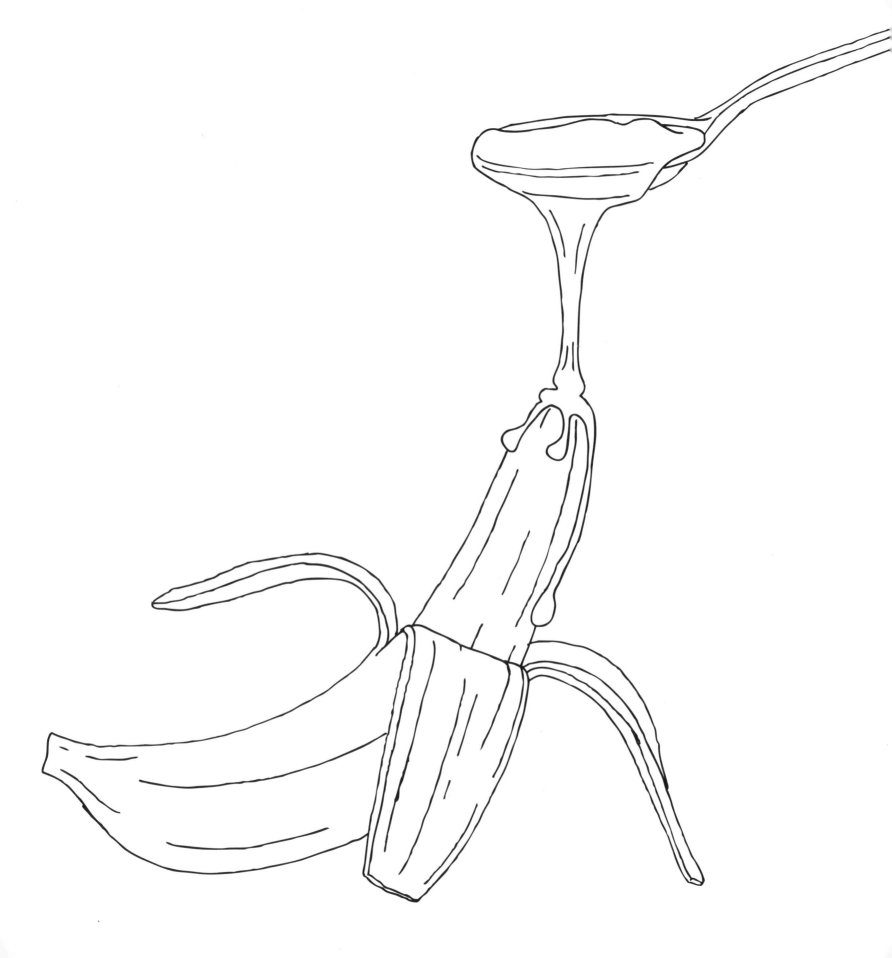

BIG BANANA FLAMBE

We like big bananas best - who doesn't? But whether yours is big or small, your dining companions will take great pleasure in eating, licking and sucking it - along with the hot, thick sauce that comes with it.

Ingredients

Measurements are approximate, so you can fly free and loose with this recipe and adjust the amounts to your taste.

1 big banana, nice and firm, just a tad under-ripe. (It will soften a bit in the preparation, so you want to start out with a fairly stiff specimen.)
¼ cup of butter
⅓ cup of brown sugar
Splash of orange juice and a few scrapes of rind
Cinnamon to taste
1 ounce rum, light or dark
Vanilla ice cream

Directions

Slice your banana in half lengthwise, and then into chunky pieces about 2" long.

Melt butter in a saucepan on low-medium heat. Stir in the orange juice, zest and brown sugar. When the mixture begins to boil, insert your banana and swirl it around for about one minute. You want it to soften just a bit with the heat, yet still remain nice and firm.

Dim the lights, set the mood, and get ready to light your fire! Add the rum and, if you are using a gas stove, gently tilt the edge of the pan toward the flame. If you are using an electric stove, use a lighter and try not to singe your knuckles! The flame will catch on the highly flammable vapor given off by the alcohol. It'll be a quickie, burning briefly but very intensely. When the flame is spent, spoon that sweet, sticky banana over a bowl of vanilla ice cream, smack your lips and dive in!

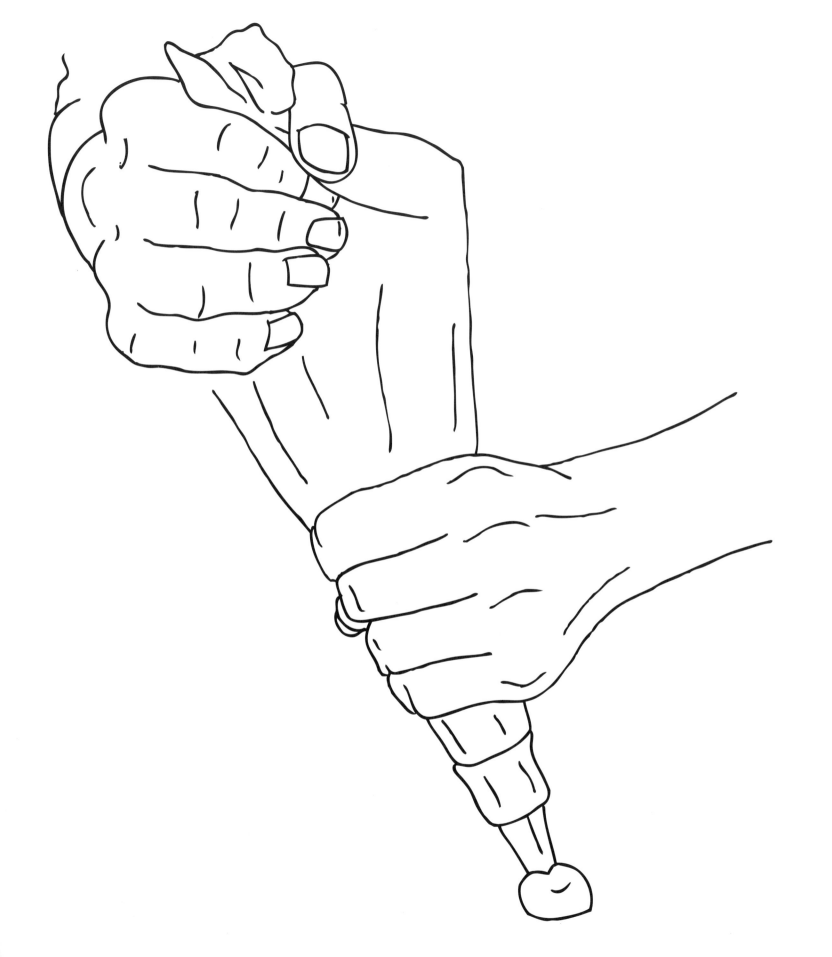

Cream Your Pants Puffs — Part I

Ingredients

- 1 cup water
- ½ cup (one stick) unsalted butter
- ¼ teaspoon salt
- 1 cup flour
- 4 large eggs

Bury your tongue in these sweet little mounds overflowing with luscious, silky cream. Then bite hard - if you're lucky, you might get a squirter!

Directions

Preheat oven to 375° F (190° C).
Mix water, butter, and salt in a small saucepan over medium heat. When it simmers, lower heat, add the flour and quickly mix with a wooden spoon for about a minute. It will turn into a mass of soft dough.

Transfer the dough into the bowl of your mixer and let it cool off. When it is cool enough to touch, mix at medium speed, adding the eggs one at a time.

If you have a pastry bag and a star tip:
Fill pastry bag with dough, then grip the bag while moving your hand in a circular motion and gently squeezing. Repeat. Repeat again. Find your rhythm… circle and squeeze, rest. Circle and squeeze, rest. You'll create 1x1 inch mounds directly on the cookie sheet, resulting in bite-sized puffs - perfect for popping in your mouth whole.

No pastry bag:
Spoon 1x1 inch balls of dough onto the cookie sheet. Take care to keep them nice and round - misshapen balls are less pleasing visually, and much harder to fill.

Bake for 20 minutes on the top rack. Remove from oven and poke each puff with a knife to release the steam. Put them back into the oven 5 minutes. This will ensure the insides are fully cooked.

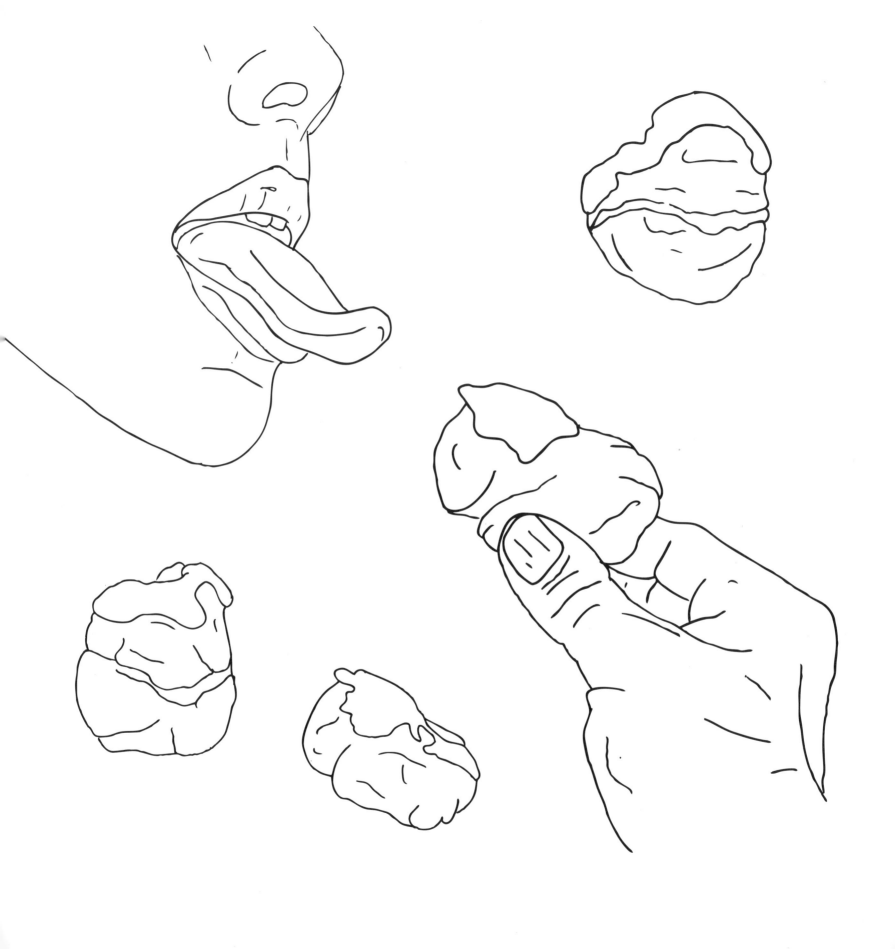

Cream Your Pants Puffs Part II

Stabilized Whipped Cream

Unless you plan to devour all your puffs right away, it's a good idea to stabilize the whipped cream filling with a touch of gelatin. It will help keep the puffs silky, moist and ready for action over a longer time.

1 teaspoon unflavored gelatin
4 teaspoon cold water
1 cup cold heavy cream
½ teaspoon vanilla extract
¼ cup confectioner's sugar

In small pan, combine gelatin and cold water; let stand until thick. Place over low heat, stirring constantly, just until gelatin dissolves. Remove from heat and cool, but don't allow it to set.

Whip the cream with powdered sugar until slightly thick. Gradually add gelatin to whipped cream while slowly beating. Whip at high speed until stiff.

Chocolate Drizzle
½ cup chocolate chips
2 tsp oil

Melt the chocolate chips in microwave or on stove, add oil and mix well.

Cream Your Puffs

Let the puffs cool for 10 minutes before cutting in half.
Add dollops of creamy filling to each puff using a piping bag or a spoon.
Be generous - the creamier, the better.
Reassemble puffs and drizzle generously with chocolate.
Finally, savor each explosion of creamy sweetness in your mouth!

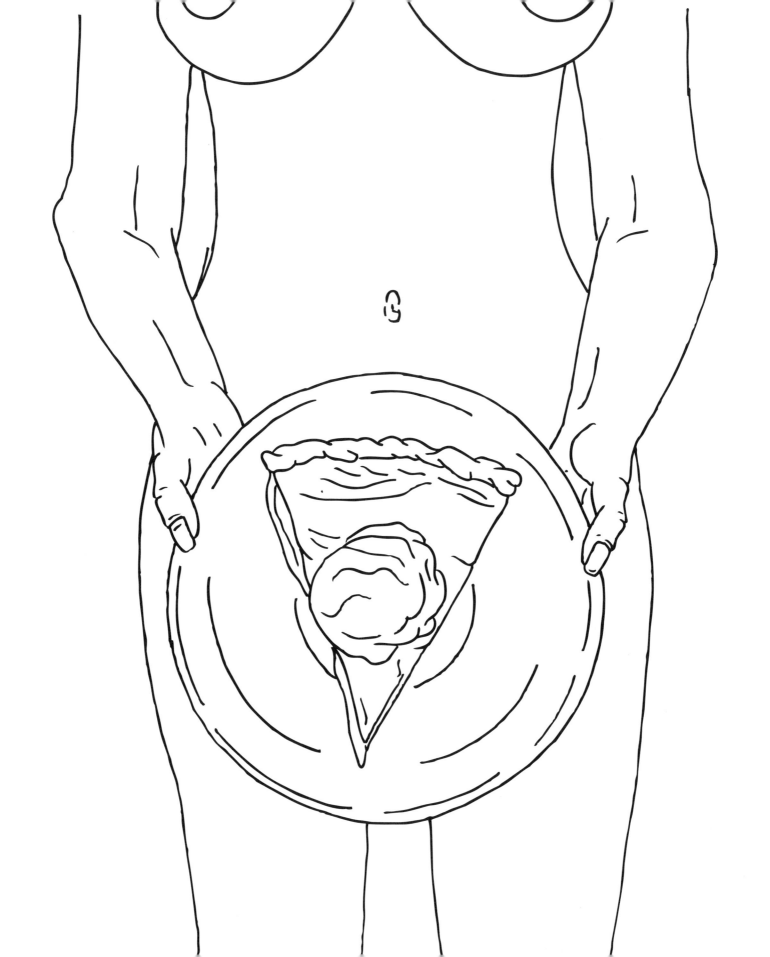

Pound the Pudding Pie

So many "recipes" these days rely on processed, packaged goods like cake mixes, but here at Suck My Cookbook, we believe in getting back to masturbasics and making things ourselves with fresh, wholesome ingredients. Take pudding, for instance. Sure, it's easy enough to buy a mix, but it just can't compare with the silky goodness and the heightened satisfaction you feel when you use a bit of elbow grease and your own hands to produce your pudding. Go ahead, take a whack at it and see if we aren't right.

Ingredients

1 9-inch pie shell, baked
2 cups white sugar (separated)
1/3 cup all-purpose flour
1/8 teaspoon salt
2 cups milk
4 egg yolks, beaten
1 cup white sugar
Whipped cream

Directions

In a medium saucepan, combine 1 cup sugar, flour, salt, milk and egg yolks, stirring until smooth. Cook over medium heat and just keep stirring steadily until your pudding creams, hot and thick with small bubbles exploding on the surface. Remove from heat and set aside.

Sprinkle remaining 1 cup sugar in a 10-inch skillet. Stir continuously over medium heat. As the temperature of the sugar slowly but surely builds, just go on stirring with a steady rhythm until the sweet crystals reach their peak and burst into streams of luscious caramel. Remove from heat and quickly pour into the warm pudding mixture, gently stirring until smooth. Be quick, as the caramel will harden as it cools- and this is one time you don't want a stiffie.

Once thoroughly mixed, pour the creamy caramel filling into the pie shell and chill completely. When it's time to serve, blast a load of whipped cream all over the top and savor your handiwork!

Cocksucker Pucker Cake

Bite into this intensely lemon pound cake and experience an instant mouth climax of tart and sweet. It's kind of like receiving the best oral sex of your life while sucking on a lemon drop. Exaggeration? Perhaps just a little. But it is really fucking good!

For an extra tangy bang, be sure to drizzle the succulent lemon syrup generously over the finished cake, and prepare to pucker up!

Ingredients

½ pound unsalted butter
2 cups sugar
2 tablespoons lemon zest
2 tablespoons lemon juice
3 eggs
1 cup buttermilk
3 cups flour
½ teaspoon baking soda
1 teaspoon salt

Directions

Preheat oven to 350° F (175° C). Have butter, eggs and buttermilk at room temperature. Cream butter and sugar with an electric mixer until fluffy and smooth. Mix in lemon zest and juice, then eggs one at a time.

In a separate bowl, sift and combine dry ingredients. On lowest mixing speed, add half the dry ingredients, then the buttermilk, then the rest of the dry.

Get a 10-incher nice and greased up - a tube pan, that is. Pour in batter and bake 60-65 minutes or until cake is springy to the touch. Thrust a toothpick in the center and if it comes out clean, the cake is ready.

Don't have buttermilk? Just combine 1 cup milk with 1 tablespoon lemon juice and let it sit 5 minutes.

Lemon Syrup

Ingredients

1 cup fresh lemon juice
⅔ cup sugar
¼ cup water
Zest of 1 lemon

Directions

Combine all ingredients and heat until the syrup is reduced by about half. Pour ½ of the syrup on the cake while just out of the oven, still in the pan. Invert the cake onto a plate on a cooling rack and drizzle with remaining syrup.

This cake is equally mindblowing when using oranges or tangerines in place of the lemons.

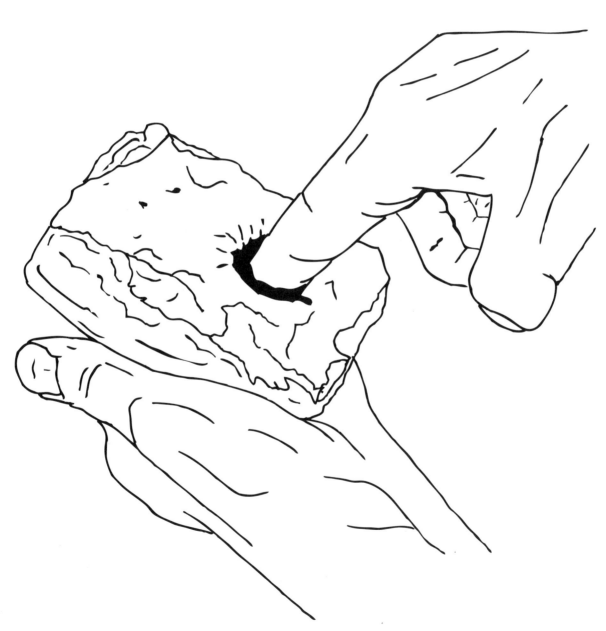

Up the Butterscotch Brownies

there's a lot to take in

So sweet, so rich, so decadent…
this dessert can be intense - particularly for the uninitiated!

If you're a Butterscotch Brownie virgin, we suggest you take things slow. Start with a very small morsel and ease your way up to a one-inch piece, then a two-inch piece, and so on until you reach the ideal size for you. If your mouth is a bit dry, a little milk to lubricate your lips will help that brownie slide right in. Then give your senses time to adjust, as the dark chewy chocolate and thick drizzle of butterscotch send tingles from your tongue to every inch of your body.

Brownies

2 ounces unsweetened baking chocolate
2 ounces semi-sweet baking chocolate (can use 3 tablespoons chocolate chips as long as they do not contain vegetable oil).
¾ cup unsalted butter
1¼ cups sugar
3 eggs
1 tablespoon vanilla extract
2 tablespoons unsweetened cocoa powder. If you are already experienced with rich chocolate, try Special Dark for an even deeper flavor.
¼ teaspoon salt
1 cup all-purpose flour
¾ cup mini chocolate chips

Salted Butterscotch

1 cup brown sugar
½ cup heavy whipping cream
6 tablespoons butter
1 teaspoon vanilla
1½ teaspoons kosher salt

Directions

Preheat oven to 350º F (175º C). Line a 9x9" pan with foil and spray with cooking spray.

Place the baking chocolate and butter in a large, microwave-safe bowl. Heat on HIGH in 30-second bursts, stirring after each, until chocolate is smooth. Add sugar and stir until incorporated, then add eggs, vanilla, and cocoa and combine well. Carefully fold in the flour, and then the mini chocolate chips.

Spread brownie batter in prepared pan and bake for 25-30 minutes. To test for doneness, plunge a toothpick into the center and withdraw it quickly. It should come out with just a few crumbs stuck to it.

While the brownies are baking, make the butterscotch sauce. Melt the butter in a saucepan over medium heat. Add the brown sugar and whipping cream and stir until it boils. Once it boils, let it continue to cook without stirring for 3 minutes. Remove from heat, then stir in vanilla and 1½ teaspoons salt. Transfer to a jar and let it cool on the counter until the brownies are done.

When brownies are fresh out of the oven and still hot, immediately top with ¾ cup of the butterscotch sauce. Let cool completely before slicing. The heat of this dish is so intense that it will take several hours to cool at room temperature. Chill brownies in the fridge if you're in a rush.

You will have plenty of extra butterscotch sauce for drizzling on sundaes - or tasty companions. It can be kept sealed for up to one week. It will stay semi-hard on the counter, and will fully stiffen in the refrigerator. Just warm it up 10-30 seconds in the microwave to return it to a sweet, slick liquid state.

Whip It Mousse
White Chocolate with Sticky Mango Sauce

Enjoy the flick of a whip from time to time, do you? Want to achieve the stiff peaks of a silky white mousse, and then lick it up from all nature of creative places? Yeah... us too.

That's why this recipe is an absolute favorite. It's incredibly simple and can be whipped up quite handily. The sweet, sticky mango sauce is also easy, yet quite impressive when dripping down the mounds of creamy mousse. You'll be lapping it up in no time!

Ingredients
1 pint whipping cream, divided
4 ounces white chocolate bar or chips
3 tablespoons triple sec (optional)

Directions
In a small sauce pan, heat ½ cup of whipping cream until simmering. Place white chocolate in a heat-proof bowl and pour the simmering cream over top. Mix until the chocolate is evenly melted and the mixture is smooth. Set aside to cool.

Pour the remaining pint (about 1½ cups) into a stand mixer and whisk on high until stiff peaks begin to form. Pay close attention anytime you are whipping something (or someone), because if you take things too far then everything simply breaks down.

Carefully fold the cooled white chocolate mixture into the whipped cream. Fold in liqueur, if desired. Refrigerate for 2 hours before serving.

Mango Sauce
1 mango, peeled and chopped (fresh if possible, but frozen will work)
½ cup orange juice
2 tablespoons lime juice
2 tablespoons triple sec (optional)

Blend everything until smooth.

Drizzle the tangy nectar over the swells of creamy white mousse, then take the plunge with your tongue!

Crossword

All these phrases are titles to our recipes. Look through the book to find the matching recipe to fill in the blank!

ACROSS:
3. _____ Colada
5. _____ y Guacahole
7. Hot _____ (drink)
8. Smell my _____ Potatoes
9. _____ Pork Sandwich
10 Savory ___ Chowder
11. Jamaican Me _____ Chicken
14. _____ Pot Pie
15. _____ Punch
16. _____ Pie

DOWN:
1. Roasted Asparagus _____
2. _____ Mojito
4. Up The _____ Brownies
6. _____ Puffs
7. _____ Flambé
8. Why Don't You _____ Me
9. Little Caesar _____
12. Morning ____ Muffins
13. Hot and Creamy _____

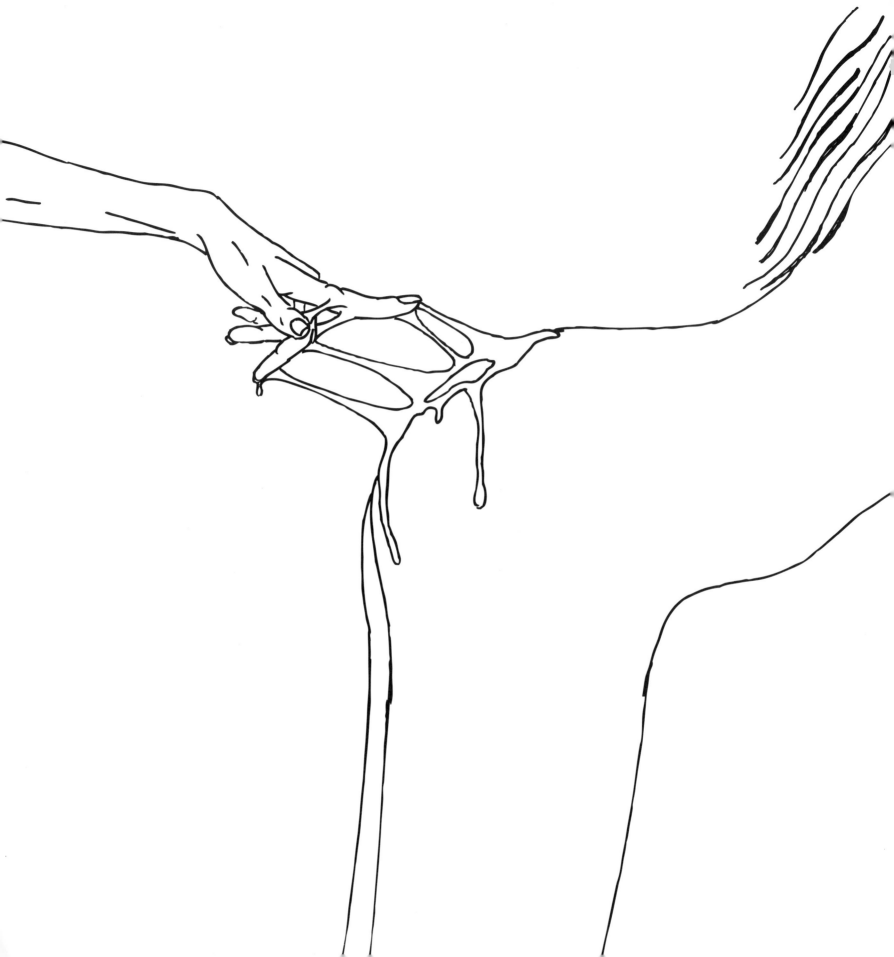

Sticky Buns

If there is anything more alluring than hot, sweet, sticky buns,
it's hot, sweet, sticky buns that are EASY - and these are as easy as they come.
We're using frozen puff pastry as a shortcut to get you off to sticky bun nirvana faster
than you can shake your stick, and you won't be able to keep your hands off them . . .
not to mention your mouth!

Ingredients

Topping

6 tablespoons softened butter
⅓ cup brown sugar, packed
½ cup pecan pieces

Buns

1 package (17 ounces, 2 sheets) frozen puff pastry, thawed
⅔ cup brown sugar, packed
3 teaspoons cinnamon
½ teaspoon grated nutmeg
1 cup raisins (optional)

Directions

Preheat the oven to 350º F (175º C) with a rack in the middle position. Beat the softened butter with ⅓ cup brown sugar until light and fluffy. Divide between 12 muffin cups, then evenly sprinkle pecans on top.

Combine ⅓ cup brown sugar, cinnamon, and nutmeg. Unfold one sheet of puff pastry and evenly sprinkle half of the brown sugar mixture on top, leaving a 1-inch border. Add half the raisins, if using.

Tightly roll the pastry sheet, jelly roll style. Slice off the unsightly ends, then slice roll into 6 evenly sized pieces. Do the same with other pastry sheet and you will have 12 cute buns, filled with sugar, spice and everything nice!

Insert each roll into a waiting muffin cup, cut side down, right on top of the butter, sugar, and pecan mixture. Bake for 25 minutes, until rolls puff up and turn golden brown. Flip the muffin tin upside down over a tray to release the pastries, scooping out any lingering luscious goo and drizzling it over the top. Let cool 5 minutes, then bury your face in these hot buns!

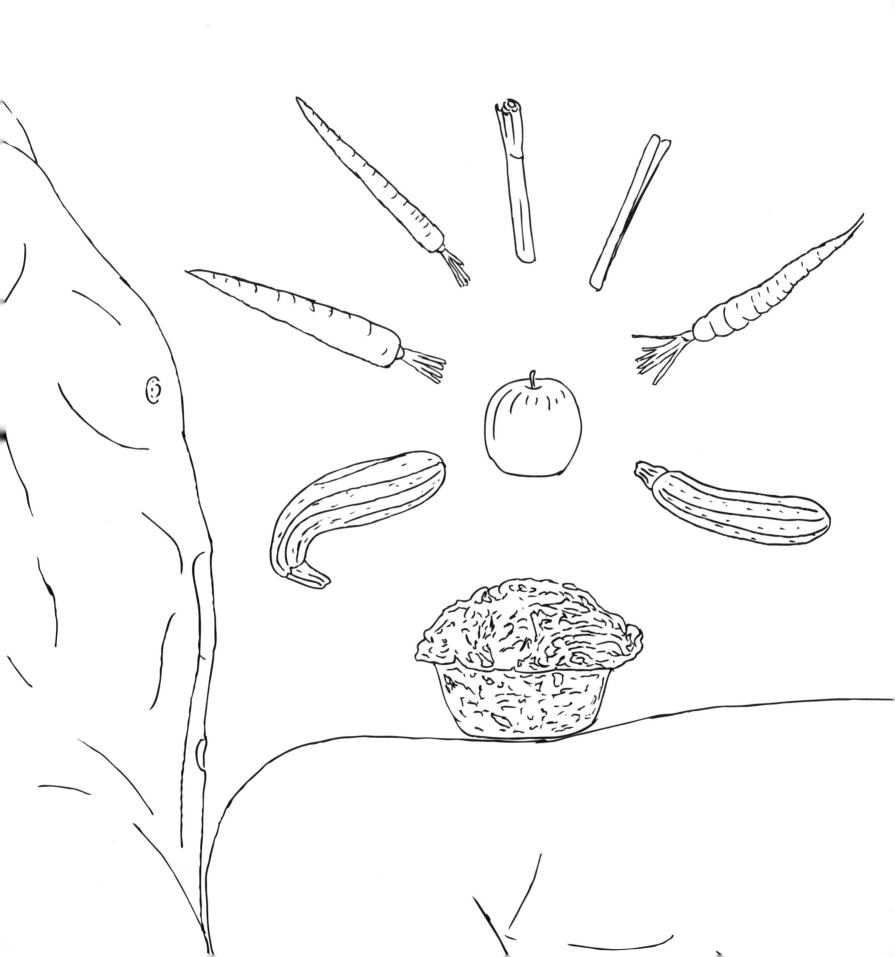

Morning Orgy Muffins

Set an alarm - you'll want to wake up early for this party! Dive into this rapturous fusion of veggies, fruits, and nuts, interwoven together so intimately that you can't tell where one ends and the next begins. One bite, and you'll experience multiple simultaneous taste sensations that will flood your pleasure center with bliss.

It's one big, ecstatic celebration of taste and texture, and you are invited! Yumm!

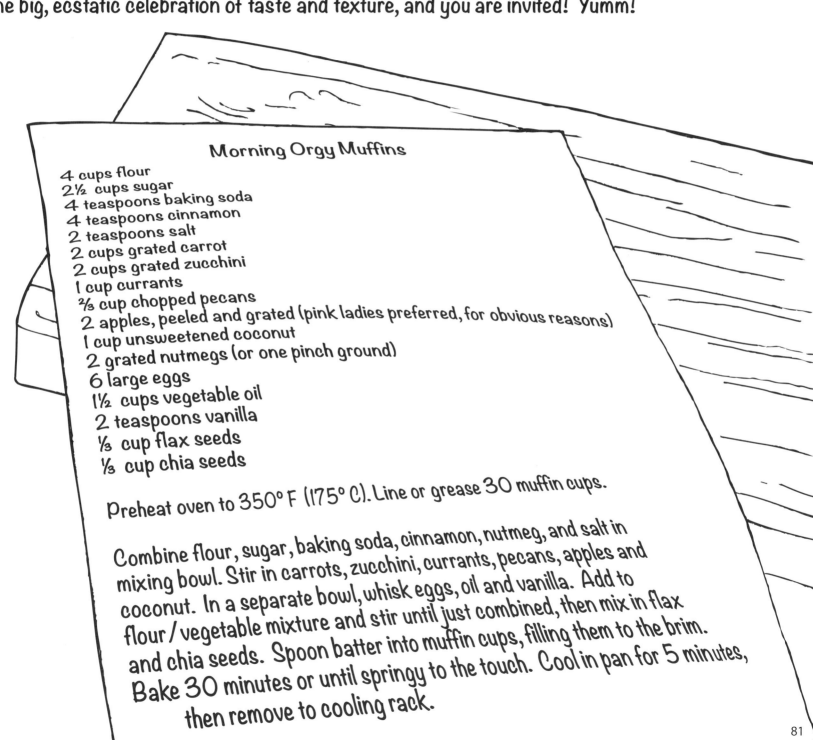

Morning Orgy Muffins

- 4 cups flour
- 2½ cups sugar
- 4 teaspoons baking soda
- 4 teaspoons cinnamon
- 2 teaspoons salt
- 2 cups grated carrot
- 2 cups grated zucchini
- 1 cup currants
- ⅔ cup chopped pecans
- 2 apples, peeled and grated (pink ladies preferred, for obvious reasons)
- 1 cup unsweetened coconut
- 2 grated nutmegs (or one pinch ground)
- 6 large eggs
- 1½ cups vegetable oil
- 2 teaspoons vanilla
- ⅓ cup flax seeds
- ⅓ cup chia seeds

Preheat oven to 350° F (175° C). Line or grease 30 muffin cups.

Combine flour, sugar, baking soda, cinnamon, nutmeg, and salt in mixing bowl. Stir in carrots, zucchini, currants, pecans, apples and coconut. In a separate bowl, whisk eggs, oil and vanilla. Add to flour/vegetable mixture and stir until just combined, then mix in flax and chia seeds. Spoon batter into muffin cups, filling them to the brim. Bake 30 minutes or until springy to the touch. Cool in pan for 5 minutes, then remove to cooling rack.

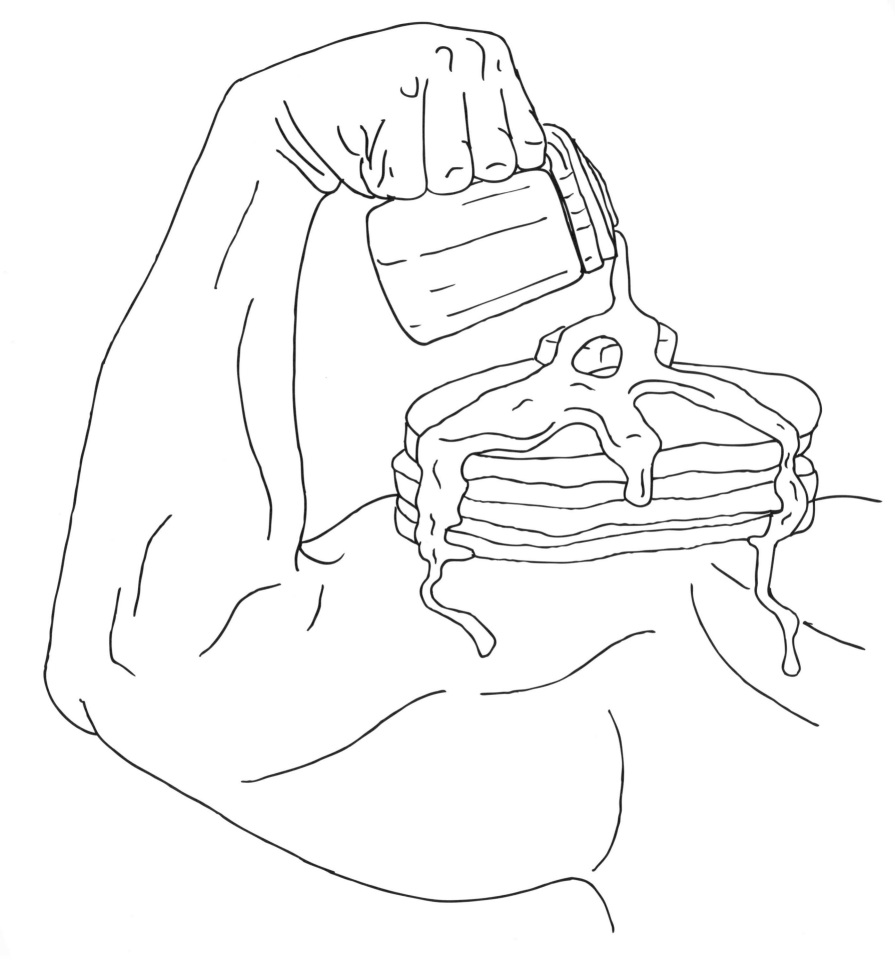

MANLY MANCAKES

For the fella who has blown his morning wood and needs a pick me up for round two, we've got hearty buckwheat pancakes packed with nuts for protein, a big banana for inspiration, and a pinch of cayenne for increased blood flow in all the right places.

Of course, dudes aren't the only ones who need to keep their strength up. While we admittedly had boners on the brain when con-cock-ting this recipe, these hotcakes will help keep passion pumping for the ladies as well.

INGREDIENTS

Vegetable oil to coat the pan
1½ cup buckwheat flour
3 tablespoons sugar
¼ teaspoon salt
1 teaspoon baking soda
1½ teaspoon baking powder
3 tablespoons unsalted butter, melted
2 eggs, beaten
2 cups buttermilk
   *Don't have buttermilk? Just combine 2 cups milk with 2 tablespoons lemon juice or white vinegar and let it sit 5 minutes.
2 big bananas, cut into ½ inch pieces
¼ - ½ cup nuts (walnuts or pecans work well)
1 cup pure maple syrup
½ teaspoon ground cayenne pepper

DIRECTIONS

Whisk together the dry ingredients in a large bowl. Stir in the melted butter.

Combine the beaten eggs with 1 cup of the buttermilk and the chopped bananas. Add this to the dry ingredients, then slowly stir in more buttermilk until you achieve the correct consistency for the batter. Stir only until everything is combined but batter is still a bit lumpy - do not over-mix! Fold in nuts.

Heat a well-seasoned griddle or skillet on medium heat. Test temperature by flicking a splash of water on the pan - if it sizzles, you're good to go. Coat the pan or griddle with about ½ teaspoon of vegetable oil.

Ladle the batter onto the hot surface to the desired size, about 4-5 inches wide. (A ¼ cup measure will ladle about a 4-inch mancake.) Reduce the heat to medium-low. After 2 or 3 minutes, watch for air bubbles along the edge of the cakes. When they start to rise in the center of the pancake, flip it and cook for another 1-2 minutes, or until nicely browned. Spread more oil on the pan as needed between batches.

In a glass bowl, combine syrup with cayenne pepper and stir well. Heat in the microwave for 15-30 seconds, drench your cakes, and man up!

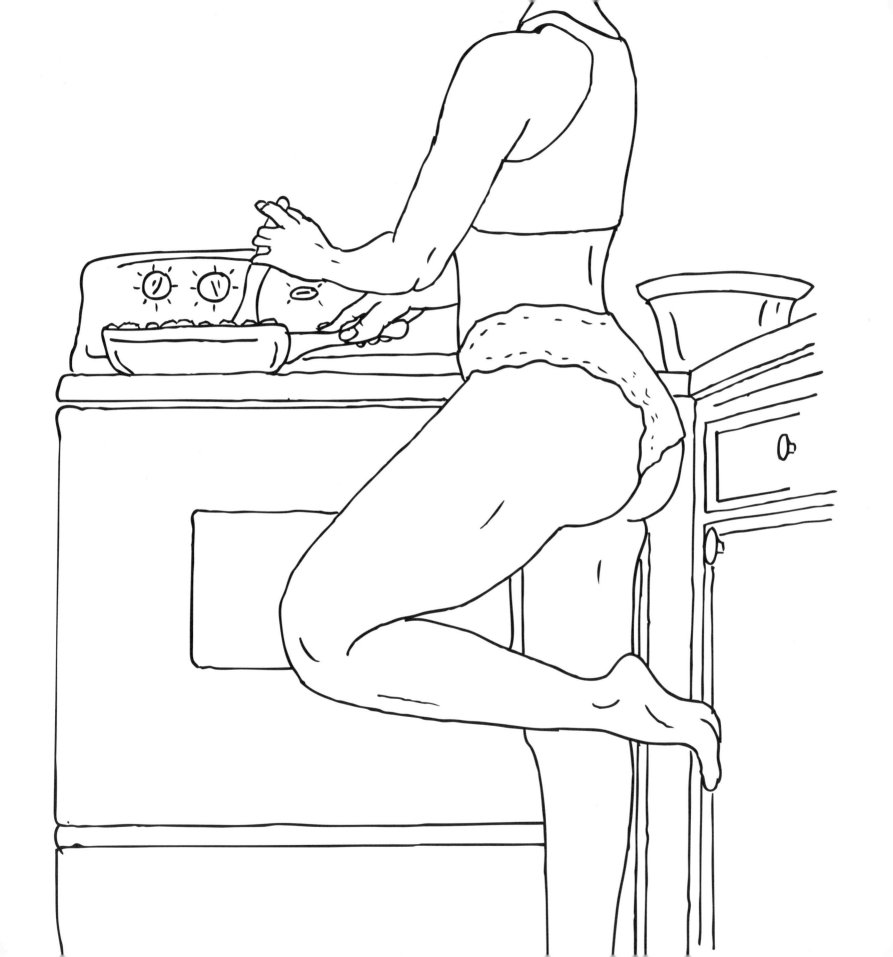

SLAMMIN' HAM 'N EGGS

We like to call this our
Slam Bam, Thank You Ma'am breakfast!
Slap this ham, eggs and jalapeño dish together and
indulge in a sizzling hot morning bang!

Ingredients

8 eggs
3 tablespoons milk
¼ teaspoon salt
ground black pepper to taste
¼ cup olive oil
1 jalapeño pepper, seeded and minced
¾ cup ham, chopped or cubed
1 cup shredded Mexican blend cheese, divided

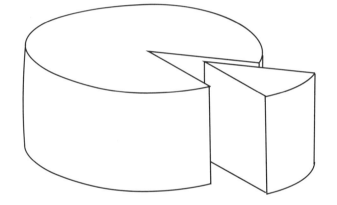

Directions

Combine eggs, milk, salt, and black pepper together and beat them hard.

Heat olive oil in a large skillet over medium-high heat, then add jalapeño and sauté until slightly softened, 2-3 minutes. Add ham to jalapeño and cook until heated through, about 1 minute. Pour egg mixture into ham mixture. Cook and stir until eggs are set but not dry, 3-5 minutes.

Sprinkle ½ of the cheese over eggs; cook and stir until cheese is melted. Transfer eggs to a serving platter and sprinkle remaining cheese over the top.

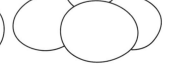

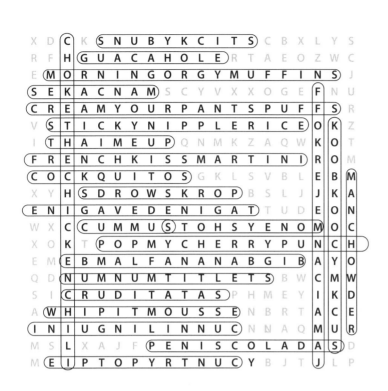
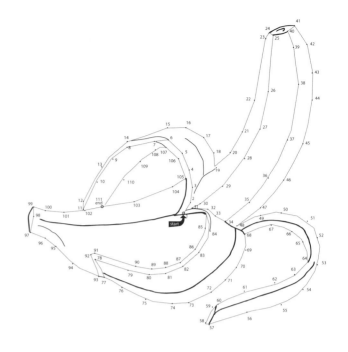
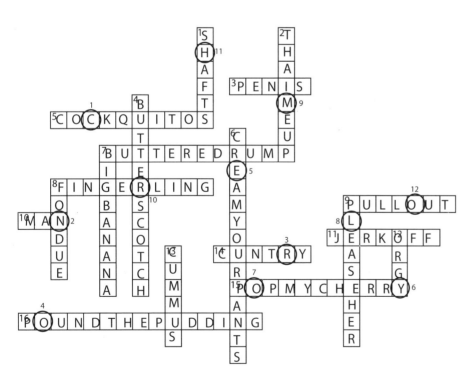
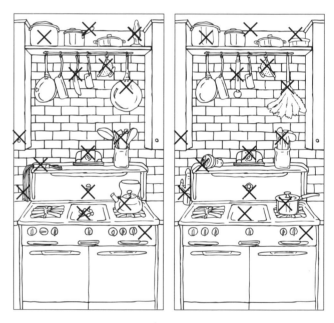
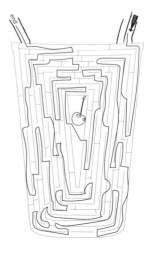

COLOR ME HORNY
1 12 8 4 3 9 5 11 7 10 2 6